Penguin

Animal
Series editor: Jonathan Burt

Penguin

Stephen Martin

REAKTION BOOKS

Published by
REAKTION BOOKS LTD
33 Great Sutton Street
London EC1V 0DX, UK
www.reaktionbooks.co.uk

First published 2009
Copyright © Stephen Martin 2009

Printed and bound in China by Eurasia

British Library Cataloguing in Publication Data
Stephen Martin, 1951–
    Penguin. – (Animal)
    1. Penguins 2. Animals and civilization
    I. Title
    598.4′7

ISBN: 978 1 86189 376 5

Contents

Introduction

One afternoon in early 2008 a group of us sat in a rubber dinghy near the tourist ship *Marina Sveteava*. Fog enshrouded nearby Macquarie Island and enclosed us in a space that included the zodiac, the ship and a lot of King penguins. Dozens of these birds surrounded the zodiac. Black, yellow and white, they swam easily through the water, surfacing beside the rubber pontoons of the craft to peer inquisitively at the people. Then turning, the penguins dived and flew away, colours bright against the sea. It was an extraordinary group in the zodiac. Historians, travellers, scientists, tour guides, all with many trips to Macquarie Island in their experience, most with voyages further south. We were familiar with penguins and the special Macquarie Island welcome. But, once again, we were entranced. Standing on the decks of the ship, observers commented on the childlike smiles and sense of wonderment they saw on our faces. It's an enchanting 'welcome' to one of the world's most remote places. These penguins entertain and intrigue the human visitor, leaving us bemused, touched by a sense of the familiar and the exotic.

Why such interest in penguins? For some of the answer, we can go back to 1895, when W. H. Bickerton sailed on the brig *Gratitude* to Macquarie Island, accompanied by a gang of men who were to continue the trade in penguin oil – killing penguins

King penguin diving off Macquarie Island, Southern Ocean, 2004.

and rendering their bodies down for oil. In an article published in the popular *Pall Mall Magazine*, Bickerton described his contact with the penguins in terms that were then and still remain as standard ways of seeing penguins. Soon after the arrival of the *Gratitude*, it was 'surrounded by the birds, who in their anxiety to fathom the mystery of the strange creature who had invaded their territories, lifted themselves almost out of the water'. After a short stay on Macquarie Island, Bickerton summed up his impressions of the penguins:

> Never while I was on the island with these birds around me did the time drag heavily away, and I cannot feel that this was mainly due to the interest (one almost says companionship) of the penguins . . . there was something in their grouping . . . which affected me strangely, and reminded me of knots of men. Perhaps it is the impression of similarity which has led me to write about them more as if they were a nation of people than a mass of multitudinous birds fulfilling nature's laws.[1]

There *is* something about penguins that connects us to them. The writer William L. Fox includes them in the body of 'charismatic animals' that inhabit Antarctica. George Gaylord Simpson, penguin expert and enthusiast, exclaimed that 'penguins are addictive'. Nature writer Diane Ackerman, writing about her experiences of king penguins on South Georgia in the South Atlantic, observed:

> There is, ordinarily, a no-man's land between us and wild animals. They fear us and shy away. But penguins are among the very few animals on earth that cross that divide. They seem to regard us as penguins, too . . . After

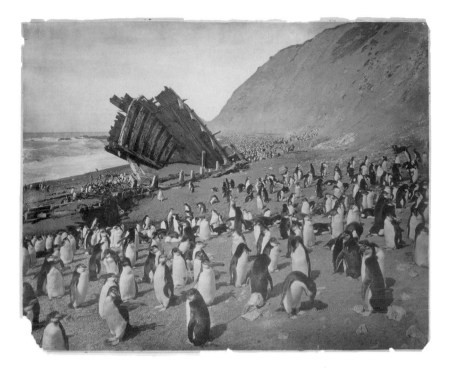

all, we stand upright, travel in groups, talk all the time, sort of waddle.[2]

The idea of penguin in human culture is as old as human communities near penguin habitats, or, to be more specific, in the landed sections of penguin habitats, since penguins spend a large proportion of their lives at sea. Indigenous accounts, such as exist, include penguins as small, inoffensive animals, their skins sometimes useful as clothing and ornament and their flesh as food. With stories that date from the twelfth century, at the beginnings of European expansion, the European imagination

Wreck of the *Gratitude*, Macquarie Island, in 1911. The ship brought sealers, who slaughtered Royal and King Penguins for their oil.

began to include penguins (or great auks, as we shall see later). Compared to animals with longer human associations, however, the penguin story is relatively new. But the relationships between people and penguins – the impact of penguins on human development – are much more than early travellers' stories. Penguins were first seen as food for European sailors.

In 1578 the English sailor, explorer and sometime pirate Sir Francis Drake sailed south along the coast of Patagonia. John Winter sailed with him and left us with the following account of an encounter with penguins on St Georges Island (now called Santa Magdalena), about 25 miles north-east of Tierra del Fuego:

Here we staied one day & victualled our selves with a kinde of foule which is plentiful in that isle, and whose flesh is not farre unlike a fat goose in England: they have no wings, but short pineons which serve their turne in swimming. Their colour is somewhat blacke mixt with white spots under their belly, and about their necke. They walke so upright, that a farre off man would take them to be little children.[3]

For more than 400 years Europeans have commented on the appearance of penguins. Most of these writings and representations allude to recognizable, human-like attributes of shape or behaviour. Of all the birds the penguin is most often described and discussed in anthropomorphic terms. What makes a penguin human? At first sight, the answer is obvious: other humans. A lovely example appears in the ecologist Peter Cosier's film of 2007, *One Summer Dream*. Cosier filmed himself talking with a pair of King penguins, which seem engaged with his conversation. He spoke gently, affectionately, treating the penguins as if they were worthy of human respect. The King penguins stood

King penguins and chicks in a colony, South Georgia, Falkland Islands. This large and beautiful bird is known for its regal bearing and striking colours.

King penguin at Macquarie Island, striding out and looking remarkably human.

nearby and looked at him, seemingly listening to his words. As they turned away, Cosier wished them well. His tone was polite, and although the effect of the scene was comic, his respect was obvious. In a conversation immediately after the screening, the critic Katherine West praised his approach, saying: 'He made the penguins human.'[4]

The shape of a penguin and its upright stance are obvious points of recognition that help people to associate penguins with little people. With their streamlined shape and flippers they are the most human-like of all birds. In his wonderful paper on Emperor penguins, the scientist Edward Wilson of Scott's British National Antarctic Expedition of 1901–4 noted another appealing physical characteristic: 'the complete absence of any protrusion of the brow . . . gives the bird a quizzical look which is always entertaining'.[5] It is an image that has given birth to a thousand stories.

Recently, the Australian journalist Flip Byrnes fell in love with Antarctica. Her 'suitor' was a penguin, aptly enough a common symbol used to attract tourists to the continent. Her use of the penguin makes the following seem almost reasonable:

> he was dressed smartly in black and white, waddling across the ice-strewn stage of Neko harbour, which looked more like an underground rave with penguins. He was vertically challenged and plump, but I've never gone for looks. Perched on a rock, I tried some ESP 'Hey handsome, how about you grab this wallflower some ice for her drink?' He turned. Our eyes met across the crowded party. Time stopped.
>
> As he came my way I tried not to breathe in hope. Approaching, he snuggled next to my leg.
>
> How forward! And then pecked at my pants. How bold! Just when I thought we were about to swap numbers he turned his back and leaned against my rock. I was just a convenient windbreak.[6]

It is an association with a long history, written about many times. The Polish scientist Emile Racovitza, who with others on the *Belgica* spent the winter of 1898 stuck fast in the ice off the Antarctic Peninsula, wrote that to picture a penguin observers should imagine:

a little old man, standing erect, provided with two broad paddles, with a head small in comparison with the plump, stout body; imagine this creature with his back covered with a dark coat spotted with blue, tapering behind to a pointed tail that drags on the ground, and adorned in front with a glossy white breastplate. Have this creature walk on his two feet, and give him at the same time a droll little waddle and a continued movement of the head; you have before you something irresistibly attractive and comical.[7]

Diane Ackerman travelled south in the 1980s, and her essay on the experience was published in the *New Yorker*. Before her trip she had helped care for penguins in the famous penguin 'enclosures' of San Diego Zoo. Penguins brought out a strong 'mothering instinct in her'. She wondered about our strong responses to penguins, listing their upright stance and walk and their similarity to children; continuing:

They are very curious about humans . . . When you look down, you find an affectionate creature standing tall and straight as a young child, perhaps offering you its flipper the way we shake hands . . . they sometimes seem so much a caricature of human life. They like company but also bicker with their neighbours; they give their mate gifts of stones but also quarrel from time to time, have affairs, and divorce and remarry; they're affectionate, attentive parents and share the child rearing; they live in colonies that function like cities; they're plagued by adolescent gangs . . . If someone were to design an adorable animal that acted enough like a human being to be endearing but was different enough also to be exotic, a penguin would do perfectly.[8]

16

The sartorial familiarity of penguins needs no introduction. In a recent article on male style, the fashion consultant Ian Garlant discussed wedding clothing: 'I'm trying to think of the grander weddings I have been to lately in a morning coat . . . When done properly it looks wonderful. But I've seen so many that were appalling, the guys looked like ill formed penguins.'[9] Many accounts have taken the penguin–human relationship further; we often see things from the penguins' point of view, as did Diane Ackerman in her description of a penguin in the San Diego Zoo:

> Life would be artificial of course, but also much safer . . . safe from hunger, leopard seal, and skua, he [the penguin] was probably sitting like a pensioner on a park bench as he watched the silent pageant passing on the moving sidewalk beyond the glass, where ghostly humans floated in a darkness deep as the Antarctic night.[10]

Sometimes, like the veteran penguin researcher Bernard Stonehouse, people assume that penguins think that people are penguins: 'I have had the impression that to penguins, man is just another penguin – different, less predictable, occasionally violent, but tolerable company when he sits still and minds his own business.'[11]

In the fictional realm this relationship gets even closer. The novel *Forbush and the Penguins* tells of a scientist, Richard Forbush, who observes an Antarctic rookery of penguins alone for a long period. He identifies so closely with the penguins that he seems to become one himself.[12] Modern stories have reached what must surely be the physical limits of such human–penguin connections. In 1996 the Russian novelist Andrey Kurkov published *Death and the Penguin*. The main character, Viktor, buys a King penguin, Misha, from a financially stressed zoo. Misha falls ill and, after a visit to the vet, Viktor finds out that he needs a heart transplant. The bird is given the heart of a child killed in an accident.[13]

The idea of domestic penguins is unfamiliar. A penguin is not a chicken, although it has often been used as a source of food, neither is it a crow, a bird with long and complex links with human communities. Stories and representations of penguins are of benign, inoffensive birds. The penguin is not dangerous to humans; stories of killer – or even evil – penguins are usually concocted in contrast to the prevailing stereotype, a plucky, curious, inoffensive humanoid. To emphasize the obvious, a penguin is not a tiger or a wolf. Human societies have not lived in fear of penguin attacks. There are no theories of early humans crouching in caves desperate to avoid death or injury from penguin predation. There are, however, stories of a close, even companionable relationship between people and penguins. Many of these are

Magellanic penguin standing at its burrow, Sea Lion Island, Falkland Islands. Early mariners likened the burrows to those of rabbits.

Frozen penguin eggs at Scott Hut, Cape Evans, Ross Island, collected for food during Scott's Expedition, 1901–4.

oddities told as examples of the strangeness of things. They contain a tone of fondness or respect for the bird, an acceptance of its difference, together with affection for its manner.

The attraction of penguins is not only a wilderness reaction. In Manly, Sydney, a small but well-protected colony of Blue penguins survives in a densely populated area. They look after themselves well, but 'wardens' also protect the birds. Nominated by local authorities and self-appointed, these guardians keep dogs, cats, rats and interfering humans away from the birds and their nesting places. The local newspaper, the *Manly Daily*, appreciates the magic of the story and regularly reports on the progress of local birds, particularly those that fall ill, or are wounded and brought back to health by humans, and which are then released into the 'wild' – usually a nearby surf beach. Fittingly, the colony's exact location is a closely guarded secret.

Colonies of penguins exist near, or in the case of Sydney, within cities. These colonies, ostensibly wild, provide their human neighbours with a rich fund of symbolism, sign and story. Like other urban non-pet animals, they bridge the divide between 'pet' and 'wild'. Unlike birds such as rock pigeons, sparrows and mynah birds, penguins require greater – both legislative and community – care. (Their nests are on the ground and are therefore more susceptible to dogs, rats and cats, and since they cannot fly they are easily caught away from the water.) It is a relationship that breeds its own particular sense of familiarity and exoticism, a role particularly apposite for the penguin.

Attempts have been made, with differing degrees of success, to capture, transport and keep penguins. Stories from these experiences reflect on the attitudes of penguins towards each other throughout their known history and illustrate the changing complexities of our relationship with this exotic bird.

The story of the first European contact with penguins is laced with confusion and misinterpretation. The first penguins were not really what we now call penguins; they were great auks, now extinct. The great auk, a flightless bird that stood upright and lived in rookeries on remote northern islands and coasts, was first seen by fishermen and sailors. Although not genetically related to the penguin, it looked like one, and occupied a corresponding environmental niche to penguins in the southern hemisphere. It is probable that Spanish fishermen or Basque whalers frequented the Newfoundland fishing banks as early as the middle of the fifteenth century. The official discovery of Newfoundland was made in 1497 by John Cabot at the behest of the English king, Henry VII. About 90 years later Captain Edward Hayes of the *Golden Hind* wrote this of the great auks:

> We had sight there of an island named Penguin, of a fowl there breeding in abundance almost incredible, which cannot fly, their wings not able to carry their body, being very large (not much less than a goose) and exceeding fat: which the French men use to take without difficulty upon

Museum specimens of a Great Auk (the first species to be called penguin), photographed by Norrie of Fraserburgh, c. 1900.

that island, and to barrel them up with salt. But for lingering of time we had made us there the like provision.[14]

The great auk is now extinct, but within recorded memory it lived in great numbers around the North Atlantic. They were black and white birds, with a conspicuous white patch between the bill and the eye. They could not run, climb or fly, and if cut off from the sea they became easy prey. Sailors ate both the meat – opinions vary as to the tastiness – and the eggs. The skins and fat of the great auks were also used.

A map of 1615 by Joris van Spilbergen, showing Penguin Island in the Magellan Straits. As a locatable food source, penguins often featured on maps.

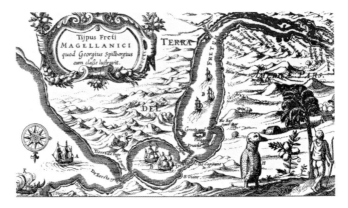

The confusion between auks and penguins continued into the twentieth century. In the late 1930s great auks were reported as living around the Lofoten Islands in Norway. On closer inspection, they were identified as King penguins, nine of which were released there in August 1936. At least two of these birds survived until 1944. The puzzlement was not confined to the boundaries between the two species. Not surprisingly, given the habitat and shape of penguins, the very nature of the bird was open to confusion. For example, as late as 1859 William Jones Rhees, writing the guide to the Smithsonian Institute display cases, noted (for Case 45) that: 'penguins are said to unite in themselves the men, fowls and fishes. Like men, they are upright; like fowls, they are feathered; and like fish, they have a fin'.[15]

Penguin cookery has no doubt been discussed since the first time penguins and their eggs were taken. The flesh has been described variously as tasting like beef or, if the fat is cooked with the meat, like fish. The penguin, while seen as an entertaining companion by most, was also a source of nutrition and in extreme circumstances the only source of food and therefore essential to survival.

The word penguin is thought by some to derive from the Welsh words *pen* (head) and *gwyn* (white). This explanation also carries connotations of political possession. A sixteenth-century advocate for Western expansion, Sir George Peckham, compiled a 'True Reporte' of the annexation of Newfoundland by Sir Humphrey Gilbert in 1583. (As early as 1566 Gilbert had written about the possibility of opening up trade with the East, believing in the existence of a northerly passage to the fabled Cathay.) The report told of 'Madock ap Owen Gwyneth' (Madog ab Owain Gwynedd), a Welsh prince who had sailed from Britain in 1170 to Newfoundland and then returned home. He named 'certain Islands, beastes, and foules under Welsh names, as the Iland of Penguin . . . There is likewise a foule in the saide countreys called by the same name at this day, and is as much to say in England, as Whitehead, and in trueth the said foules have white heads'. Peckham's writing explaining the

Great Auk: an aquatint by J. J. Audubon and R. Havell from Audubon's *The Birds of America* (1827–38).

evidence of Welsh/English visitation to the region was to 'shew the lawfull title which the Queenes most excellent Majestie hath unto those Countries'.[16]

According to another theory, the original name was *pen-wing*, with reference to the rudimentary wings of both great auks and penguins. A third theory is that penguin comes from the Latin *pinguis* ('fat'). Spanish sailors of the seventeenth century called the birds *pengüigo*, meaning grease. The Spanish now use the word *pingüino*, the Portuguese *pingüim*, the German *Penguin*, the Italian *pinguino*. The eighteenth-century French naturalist the Comte de Buffon, keen not to confuse the names of the two species, proposed the word *manchot* (meaning one-armed) for southern penguins. This word stuck, but the French also use *pinguoin*.

The etymology of penguin names could take a whole chapter. For example, gentoos were commonly called jonnies. But there are added mysteries to its name. Gentoo means 'pagan' in Hindustani; the word is believed to be of Anglo-Indian/Portuguese origin and somehow related to stories of dancing girls, but its origin is unclear. As for the gentoo's scientific name, *papua*, the first stuffed specimens to reach Britain were thought to come from the island of New Guinea; *papua* was the Malay word for 'curly'. Nothing about this penguin merits this description, so perhaps it is simply a reference to its supposed place of origin.

Of course, there are many colloquial or localized names for penguins. Eighteenth-century sailors who watched them swim through the water with their legs extended behind called them 'arse feet'. Whatever the derivation of the name, the penguin was depicted and described as an exotic bird, an inhabitant of remote places. The first observers of southern penguins were struck by the morphological and ecological similarities between

Curiousity is a penguin trait: King penguins with a tourist's bag, Fortuna Bay, South Georgia, 2006.

the two different species, and named the southern birds penguins. The name stuck.

The 'human' qualities of penguins, their apparent lack of fear and their curiosity, facilitated a rapid accommodation of these animals into human stories. Penguins act as characters in fables, teaching us lessons on life or giving larger insights into the nature of things. In these fables penguins are engaging, even inspirational figures.

1 Penguin Facts on File

Seventy per cent of the Earth's surface is covered by oceans, yet of the nearly 9,500 species of birds in the world, only 300 are seabirds. Of these, 17 are penguins. All of them are adapted for life in cold water. Even those in low latitudes (like the Galapagos penguins) depend on cool water currents for food. The greatest concentrations of penguin species occur in cool temperate waters: New Zealand and its southern islands support seven species and the Falkland Islands five. The Antarctic regions support five, of which three, the Emperor, Adélie and Chinstrap, breed only south of the polar front. Scientifically, penguins make up the order Sphenisciformes, meaning wedge-shaped, a reference to the shape of the wings. The largest, the Emperor penguin, can weigh as much as 30 kg (65 lb). The Little Blue penguin is the smallest at 0.8 to 1.3 kg (1 lb 12 oz.–3 lb). It stands about 40 centimetres tall.

All penguins stand upright. With their streamlined shape and flippers they are the most 'human-like' in shape of all birds. They walk with their chests lifted up and their heads high, balancing their bodies in a dignified manner. Penguin legs are part of the peculiarity. They are set far back on the body and trail behind the bird when it swims. The upper leg bones are short and are aligned horizontally to the ground, so that when the bird is standing its knees are directly beneath its centre of gravity. This configuration accounts for the famous waddle.

Penguins are counter-shaded – that is, they have a white underside and a dark (mostly black) upper side. This is for camouflage. A potential predator (such as the orca and leopard seal) has difficulty when looking up in distinguishing a white penguin belly from the reflective water surface. The dark plumage on the birds' backs provides camouflage from above. Facial and chest features, such as long yellow feathers and red beaks, are their main distinguishing characteristics. Their 'coat' is a wind-proof outer shell of overlapping feathers that protects them from water and cold. Tight and compact, it gives the penguin a sleek and neat appearance. The feathers account for approximately 90 per cent of the bird's insulation. They are continuous, covering every part of the body, and are small and lance-shaped, with a collar of down at the base. They are replaced in a seasonal

A King penguin parade in Taiwan, from the *Taipei Times*, 24 January 2006.

Adélie penguins,
Antarctic
inhabitants
and possessors.

moult. During the moult, penguins are not waterproof and they remain on shore, unable to feed. It is an uncomfortable, disabling experience, which has been likened to the skin replacement of lizards. The cast feathers lie on the ground of a penguin colony like snow, caught in grass or floating on melt-water streams.

Penguins have three large webbed toes and a fourth toe at the back of the foot, above the heel. Each toe has a heavy claw that becomes useful when they move on slippery rocks, or, for those species that burrow, to dig into compact earth. The claws are so strong that on the rocks of some colonies the continual scratching of countless penguins has left permanent grooves. Usually penguins waddle along on their feet. On snow, however, they slide along, a movement called 'tobogganing', which enables them to conserve energy and move relatively fast at the same time.

The birds swim underwater by flapping their wings (flippers). These are stiff and flat, without the adaptable flight feathers of other birds. They provide the power, while the webbed feet, tucked in under the tail, are used for steering. Most penguins can stay underwater for five to seven minutes, but the largest species (the Emperor penguin) can submerge for up to eighteen minutes. The Emperor penguin dives to 630 metres (2,070 ft). Most other species do not normally go deeper than about 100 m (330 ft). The penguin's maximum swimming speed is probably about 24 kph (15 mph), but because of their small size and streamlined shape, they often seem to be travelling faster. While swimming beneath the surface, penguins 'porpoise', breaching in swift arcs like porpoises to breathe.

An Emperor penguin 'tobogganing' on the ice.

Penguins generally feed on prey captured near the surface, either close to shore or near the edge of the pack ice. In Antarctica,

the larger species feed primarily on squid and krill, while the smaller ones eat mostly krill, with some fish and squid. Penguins have an excellent sense of hearing. Their eyes are adapted for underwater vision, and are their primary means of locating prey and avoiding predators; out of water they are near-sighted.

Virtually all penguins are social and nest in colonies. Most of the breeding colonies are on small islands or isolated sections of coast, although some colonies exist near major cities, such as Sydney and Cape Town. In Antarctica, most species use open nests lined mainly with pebbles, but also other debris such as bones and feathers. The pebbles are collected from nearby beaches and moraines or are stolen from others. Further north, where the earth or packed sand is easier to dig out, and there are more predators, several species of penguin, such as the Magellanic penguin of South America, the Little Blue penguin and the Jackass penguin, nest in burrows.

Some penguin species mate for life, others for just one season. They generally raise a small brood, and the parents cooperate in caring for the clutch and for the young. During the cold season, on the other hand, the mates separate for several months. The male stands with the egg and keeps it warm, and the female goes out to sea and finds food so that when it comes home the chick will have food to eat. Once the female returns, they switch roles. Emperor penguin colonies are situated on the ice, unlike those of other penguins, which nest on land. The male emperor incubates a single egg by balancing it on top of his feet and covering it with a special brood pouch. He must stand upright and shuffle around with the egg for about two months, while his mate is out at sea feeding. If the egg hatches before the female returns to relieve him, the male can feed the newborn chick with small quantities of crop secretions containing fat and protein.

Penguin colonies are active places and the sights, sounds and smells of these places are unforgettable. Once the eggs are laid, incubation usually lasts five to six weeks. The fledging period varies quite widely and depends to some extent on the climatic severity of the colony location. Adélies and chinstraps, for example, leave the colony at about seven weeks, while the gentoo, which breeds further north in relatively less hostile conditions, leaves at approximately fourteen weeks.

All penguins are subject to predation. Those of the far south are attacked by orcas and leopard seals. Their eggs and chicks may be taken by skuas or giant petrels. Farther north, animals introduced to their habitats by humans may eat penguins and their young. Those penguins breeding near urban communities will suffer from cats, rats and dogs. All penguins are threatened to varying degrees by human impacts such as pollution.

Macaroni penguin colony, as crowded as a city, on South Georgia.

On the evolutionary chart, penguins are placed between loons and frigatebirds. They are closely related to northern flying birds such as guillemots. Penguins emerged in warm seas, before the formation of the Antarctic continent and the consequent development of the cooler southern ocean. The oldest fossil species is the New Zealand bird *Waimanu*, which lived about 65 million years ago. *Waimanu* were flightless birds with short wings adapted for deep diving in the sea. These fossils prove that prehistoric penguins were already flightless and seagoing, so their origins probably reach as far back to the period before the extinction of the dinosaurs. By the Eocene (40 million years ago) many ancestral penguin species had evolved. During the late Eocene and the early Oligocene (40 to 30 million years ago),

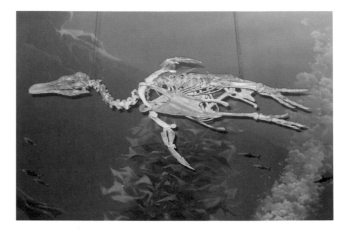

some lineages of large penguins existed. Fossils of these species have been found in New Zealand, and the former also found in Antarctica. Only during and after the Pliocene period, two to three million years ago, were penguin species likely to have encountered icy seas.

Despite finds of partial fossil skeletons, and some larger fragments, most penguin fossils are small: foot or limb bones or pieces of skull. Fossils have been found that indicate the existence of large penguin species, standing up to 1.6 m (5 ft) tall and weighing up to 80 kg (176 lb). At least one species was notably smaller than today's penguins, standing at only 0.33 m (13 in.) tall.

Discoveries of fossil deposits are stories in themselves, often because of the circumstances and reporting of their discovery, analysis and revelation. The first penguin fossil was discovered by a Maori in the late 1850s, at Kakanui, on the east coast of the South Island of New Zealand, where limestone was quarried. The fossil bone was eventually passed on to Thomas Henry Huxley at the British Museum in London. He examined the bird and in

1859 wrote an article describing the fossil: a unique, foot bone, a tarsometatarsus from the extinct penguin *Palaeeudyptes antarcticus* from the early Oligocene of about 35 million years ago.[1] The only fossil found in the Antarctic Peninsula is *Anthropornis nordenskjöeldi*, from Seymour Island. This was collected by G. Andersson during Otto Nordenskjöld's expedition of 1903–5. This giant penguin stood between 4 and 5 feet tall and may have weighed as much as 136 kg (300 lb).

In 2007 Julia Clarke, assistant professor of Marine, Earth and Atmospheric Sciences at North Carolina State University, announced the results of analysis on penguin fossils found in Peru. The fossils were of a giant penguin, *Icadyptes salasi*, which lived in warm regions of the world about 40 million years ago. It stood about 1.6 m (5 ft) tall with a long, sharp beak. News of the discovery swept around the world's media, generating headlines such as 'Peruvian Prehistoric Penguins Were Taller than Danny DeVito' and 'When Giant Penguins Roamed the Tropics'.[2] The cooler scientific descriptions of the finds remained in scientific journals.

2 Voyages of Discovery

Penguins have been a part of the human story for thousands of years. Species such as the Jackass penguin of southern Africa, the Yellow-eyed penguin of New Zealand, the Little penguin of Australasia and the Magellanic penguin of South America have lived near human communities. These peoples sometimes used penguins for food and clothing, although penguins were probably not the first choice for either. Penguins occasionally feature in indigenous stories, but not as significant or influential entities.

Penguins may have been regarded as a form of pet, a sort of half-wild but tolerated creature that lived in nearby communities. There is a report in 1868 of a New Zealand crested penguin on the Opotiki River, 'which had been captured by the natives . . . [and] was perfectly tame'.[1] According to Maori lore the islands of Aotearoa (New Zealand) were settled by men, women and animals in a series of migrations from the Pacific islands to the north-east, the legendary Hawaiki. Kupe is said to have been the first person to visit Aotearoa. When he arrived, the land had not yet assumed its present form and Kupe established landmarks and prepared the way for those who were to follow. Kupe and his companion Ngake explored the Te Wai Pounamu (South Island). When they reached the far south, Kupe told Ngake's wife, Hine-waihua, that since there were no people to be seen it would be a good place for her to leave her pet seals and penguins. She did so, and the Fiordland crested penguins have been in the region ever since.

There is another legend among Maori that Tawaki (the crested penguin) and Toroa (the albatross) were constantly arguing about which of them was better at flying and fishing. Eventually Tane Mahuta, the Lord of the Forest, grew tired of their bickering and decided to settle the matter by offering each a gift. To Toroa he gave the longest wing of any seabird so that he could sail the ocean winds far from land in search of food, and to Tawaki he gave narrow flipper wings so that he could fly beneath the ocean waves to catch all the fish he needed.

The Maori call the Little penguin Korora, and the area also known as Russell, in the North Island of New Zealand, Kororareka. Local legend has it that Kororareka is the name of a broth made from the Little Blue penguin, given to a Maori chief who had been wounded in battle. The leader is believed to have said 'How sweet is penguin'. The Maori story of Korora and the gannet is one of friendship and cooperation. Years ago the Korora lived on the land and ate worms and other small animals in the leaf litter. One day as a Korora was walking along the shore it found a gannet with a hurt wing. The gannet could not sit on its egg. The Korora offered to sit on the egg and after a few days it hatched. With its wing now healed the gannet caught small fish for both the Korora and the hatchling. The Korora developed a liking for the fish and the gannet taught it to swim and catch fish. Korora liked the new life so much that it kept to it and no longer spent much time on land. The gannet and the penguin will always be good friends.

The Maori took seabirds such as albatross and sooty petrels for food. They preserved the birds in fat, then in flaxen bags protected by an outer layer of bark. They may have treated penguins

African or Black-footed penguins, South Africa. These, the first southern penguins seen by Europeans, were nicknamed 'Jackass' because of their braying call.

in a similar manner. They knew of the Yellow-eyed penguin, which they called *hoi hoi* after its distinctive call.

The essentially animist peoples of South America may have incorporated penguins into some myths and legends. They were probably minor characters and without significant representation in indigenous art; for example, there are no penguins on pre-Colombian pottery. South American peoples like the Alacaluf and the Yahgan tribes raided penguin colonies using canoes. The Yahgan of Tierra del Fuego used the local penguins – and their eggs – mostly for food and for some clothing and items such as small bags.

The early voyages of Europeans, motivated by a search for territory and markets and often accompanied by men with a lust for curiosity, marked the beginnings of a flood of information about the world and its creatures into Europe. Many of these

La Race deuoir au deftrait de Magellâes

Early illustrators relied on non-pictorial descriptions of remote humans and wildlife, as seen here on the wall map commemorating the global voyage (1598–1601) of the Dutch navigator Olivier van Noort.

stories described new lands and strange animals. The ships often supplemented their stores with whatever the crew could catch and eat. Fresh meat was particularly sought, and the wildlife of islands at which the men stopped for both food and water was the target of indiscriminate killing for food and for sport. Like the Great Auk, southern penguins often became an important part of the seamen's diet.

Accounts of these voyages were written, published and re-published. They were read by people wanting to learn about new lands and by those who planned voyages themselves. Initially, some were anthologized in Hakluyt's famous *Voyages* and became standards of the European record. Among these accounts are the first European references to penguins, which were seen as exotic, almost marginal creatures. As such they were tokens of geography and mystery, and their images hinted at excitement and far-off places. Penguins were mysterious birds; they were unfamiliar and, being seabirds, from a different element. Often they were seen as part bird, part fish.

The first southern penguins seen by Europeans were those on the coasts of south-west Africa, now called Black-footed penguins, since this species has black feet, or Jackass penguins, because of their call. Europeans entered the range of these birds as part of the Portuguese voyages around the southern cape of Africa. In 1487–8 Bartolomeu Dias's ships rounded the tip of Africa and sailed into the Indian Ocean, proving that a passage to the Indies, and therefore access to the fabled riches, including spices, of that part of the world, was possible. The ships turned back, and on their return the men discovered and named Cape Agulhas, the southernmost tip of Africa, now known as the Cape of Good Hope. This was followed by the voyage of Vasco da Gama. On 22 November 1497 his ships rounded the cape and on 25 November entered a bay, São Braz (Sam Brás or Sanbras),

Tom. IX.

Pl. XXXI. pag. 422.

De Seve del

MANCHOT à Bec tronqué.

fine Le villain Sc.

A penguin (either African or South American) illustrated in the Comte de Buffon's *Histoire naturelle des oiseaux* (1770–85). He named the penguin *manchot*, 'one armed'.

remaining there until December. The *Roteiro*, an itinerary written by an unknown member of the crew of the *São Raphael*, describes an island full of seals and continues:

> One day, when we approached the island for our amuse-ment, we counted, among large and small ones [seals], three thousand, and we fired among them with our

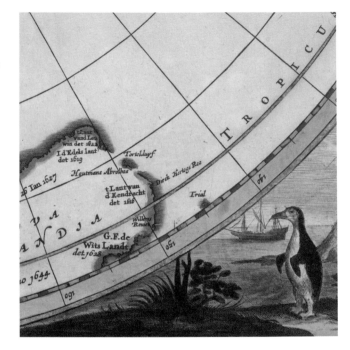

Cartographers often decorated their maps with exotic creatures, as here on Hendrik Hondius's *Polus Antarcticus*, 1637.

bombards from the sea. On the same island there are birds as big as ducks, but they cannot fly, because they have no feathers on their wings. These birds, of whom we killed as many as we chose, are called Fotylicayos, and they bray like asses.[2]

Ferdinand Magalhães (Magellan) was Portuguese by birth and served in the Portuguese navy before becoming a Spanish subject, under Charles v. Magellan persuaded the king that Spain could also be a part of the rich trade to and from the Indies. Supported by the king, Magellan planned a voyage that would go westwards around the tip of South America. With five ships, he sailed from Seville on 10 August 1519. It was the first European voyage to circumnavigate the world. Many of the crew on this expedition died, including Magellan, who was killed in a skirmish in the Philippines, but Antonio Pigafetta from Vicenza was one of the lucky ones to return home. After he

This jaunty rockhopper penguin is by John Webber, official artist on Captain James Cook's third voyage to the Pacific (1776–9).

had returned to Seville in September 1522, he wrote an account of the voyage.

The original has not survived, but translations of it give a remarkable if sometimes exaggerated account of all manner of things, including the wildlife seen by the sailors. In January 1520, on the Patagonian coast, near the mouth of the Deseado River, the ships reached two islands where the men found large numbers of penguins:

> Truly, the great number of those geese cannot be reckoned; in one hour we loaded the five ships [with them]. These geese are black and have all their feathers alike on body and wings. They do not fly, and live on fish. They were so fat that it was not necessary to pluck them but to skin them. Their beak is like that of a crow.[3]

Despite the vague description, Europeans now had news of a flightless bird that lived on the islands of southern coasts. The idea of a southern penguin had been placed in the European imagination.

Island habitats of penguins were discovered. The remote South Atlantic islands of Tristan da Cunha, 2,816 km (1,750 miles) from South Africa were first sighted by Portuguese sailor, Tristão da Cunha, in 1506. Rough seas prevented a landing, and therefore a good sighting of the northern Rockhopper that bred on the island group. Later, the many islands of the Galapagos were 'discovered' when the Dominican Fray Tomás de Berlanga, the fourth bishop of Panama, sailed to Peru. His vessels drifted off course and reached the Pacific islands in March 1535.

Penguins became standard food for many sailors. Scurvy and malnutrition haunted many voyages, and fresh penguin meat must have saved many lives. Knowledge of penguin habits grew, particularly of the times that penguins gathered at their rookeries to breed, and known rookeries became a place to replenish stores. On maps a 'penguin island' was a sign of food and, in extreme circumstances, of survival. The birds may have seemed providential to hungry sailors, particularly to those who accompanied the English sailor Thomas Cavendish, who made two voyages south, supplementing supplies with penguins. In 1586 Cavendish entered a harbour (Port Desire) in Patagonia. There was a 'great store' of penguins and seals in the vicinity. The crew killed and salted many penguins for 'victuals'. Cavendish, again with the *Desire* and with four other ships, returned to the area in 1591, this time in dire need. His ships had met with trouble and 'because famine was like to bee the best ende wee desired to goe for Port Desire, hoping with seales and penguins to relieve ourselves, and so make to Brasil'. They sailed into hard weather and after 'loftie seas' and 'dangerous foule weather', the 'foreshrouds' broke. They moored in Port Desire, where the men set up a small forge and made nails and

Restocking ships' supplies by early voyagers meant slaughtering penguins on shore.

Kerguenen Island's Christmas Harbour in the South Indian Ocean was a stopping-off point for seal- and whale-ships, where penguins were butchered for food.

bolts while others made cables; other crew members gathered mussels and penguins. On 25 October 1591,

> wee came to an Island in the Streights named Penguin-isle . . . when we came to this Isle we sent our boat on shore, which returned laden with birdes and eggs. Our men said that the penguins were so thick upon the Isle, that ships may be laden with them; they could not go without treading upon the birds.[4]

Twenty men went ashore to kill and dry penguins, and to regain their health. On 22 December, after a rest, the men loaded 14,000 dried penguin carcasses onto the *Desire*. Cavendish calculated that he needed five penguins per day for four men during the six-month journey home to England. The voyage was difficult: the water supplies ran out and, in the heat of the tropics, the penguin carcasses began to decay; worms bred throughout the supplies and into other stores of the ship. Cavendish died in the summer of 1592. In June 1593 the *Desire*, the only ship to arrive home, reached the Irish port of Bear Haven.

In 1594 Sir Richard Hawkins sailed south. He too visited Penguin Island in the Straits of Magellan, and wrote a description of the penguin and its habits:

The penguin is in all proportion like unto a Goose, and hath no fethers, but a certaine downe upon all parts of his bodie; and therefore cannot flie. But avaleth himself on all occasions with his feet, running as fast as most men. He liveth in the Sea, and on the Land, feedeth on fish in the Sea, and as a Goose on the shore upon the grasse. They harbour themselves under the Ground in Burrowes, as the Conies; and in them hatch their young. All parts of the Iland where they haunted were undermined, save only one Valley which (it seemeth) they reserved for their food; for it was as greene as any Medow in the moneth of Aprill, with a most fine short grasse. The flesh of these Pengwins is much of a certaine Fowle taken in the Ilands of Lundey and Silley, which we call Puffins, by the taste it is easily discerned that they feed on fish. They are very fat . . . they are reasonable meat rosted. We salted some dozen or sixteen Hogsheads, which served us (whilst they lasted) instead of powdred beefe.[5]

While European information about the penguin and its habits grew, so did the appetite for taking them. Penguin slaughter reached incredible heights. A few years after Hawkins, the Dutch circumnavigator Oliver van Noort came to Penguin Island 'after many tempests'. He and his crew furnished themselves with stores of penguins and fishes: 'Of those Fowles they took fifty thousand, with eggs innumerable, which proved very refreshing to the diseased.'[6]

It was a similar tale on the other side of the world. In April

APTENODYTES *chrysocoma*. APTENODYTES *antarctica*.

J. R. Forster's illustrations made on Captain Cook's second voyage (1772–5) are among the earliest attempts at accurate representations based on captured specimens. This Rockhopper (*left*) is illustrated in *Historia Aptenodytae* (1781).

A Chinstrap penguin (*right*) in Forster's *Historia Aptenodytae*.

1591 James Lancaster left Plymouth with the *Penelope*, the *Merchant Royal* and the *Edward Bonaventure*, bound for the East Indies. The ships put into a bay just short of the Cape of Good Hope for supplies, and on an island 'found great store of Penguins and Seales, whereof he brought good plenty with him'. Four years later, on 4 August 1595, during the first Dutch expedition to the East, Captain William Lodewijckszoon called at a bay near the Cape of Good Hope. Here they took many 'Pyncuins' by hand:

> We entered into a haven where we ankered and found good depth at 8 or 9 fadome water, sandy ground. We went on shore to gather fruite, therewith to refresh our sicke men . . . In this bay lyeth a small islande wherein are many birdes called Pyncuins that are taken by men's handes.[7]

But the penguin was more than an item for the stores. Travellers interested in natural history made attempts to describe this strange and confusing bird. Sir Thomas Roe, sailing around Southern Africa in 1613 on his way to present himself as Lord Ambassador to the court of the Great Mogul, attempted a classification:

> On Pengwin Island there is a fowle so called, that goes upright, his wings without feathers, hanging upside down like sleeves faced with white: they fly not, but walke in pathes and keep their divisions and quarters orderly; they are a strange fowle, or rather a miscellaneous creature, of Beast, Bird and Fish, but most of Bird, confuting that definition of man to be *Animale bipes implume*, which is nearer to a description of this creature.[8]

Sir John Narborough sailed into the Straits of Magellan in 1670. Like others before him he resupplied his vessel with seals, penguins and their eggs. His account of the expedition, published in 1694, included several references to penguins. They became well known and were often republished by others, continuing the development of a stereotype. He arrived at Penguin Island on 24 February, finding 'almost incredible' numbers of seals, seabirds and penguins. He put a boat ashore and took 300 penguins in less than an hour – and could have taken many more. On Tuesday 11 October he noted that the men were all in good health and were 'lusty and fat . . . those which had the Scurvy are got very well with the eating of Fresh Meat, and such Green Herbs as they can get on shore'. The men mixed the herbs with penguin eggs and seal oil to restore and maintain their health. In a famous and much-repeated entry, Narborough then described the penguin:

The Penguin is a Fowl that lives by catching and eating of Fish, which he dives for, and is very nimble in the Water; he is as big as a Brant Goose, and weighs near about eight Pounds; they have no Wings but flat Stumps like Fins; their Coat is a downy stumped Feather, they are blackish Grey on the Backs and Heads, and White about their Necks and down their Bellies; they are short-leg'd like a Goose, and stand upright like little Children in white Aprons, in Companies together; they are full neck-'d, and headed and beaked like a Crow, only the point of their Bills turns down a little; they will bite hard, but they are very tame, and will drive in Herds to your Boat side like Sheep, and there you may knock them on the head, all one after the another; they will not make any great haste away.[9]

By the middle of the eighteenth century new views of the natural world had developed in Europe. As a result of the many voyages to new lands, including those into penguin habitats, a steady flow of ideas, descriptions and natural history specimens was returned to home ports. In concert with these changes there grew a hunger for the new and the exotic. Since the end of the seventeenth century more rational explanations of the world and its life had been expressed and espoused in personal communications and at forums like the Royal Society of London, established in 1660. As part of the new perceptions, natural histories continued to describe the penguin and to place it both geographically and within a conceptual framework of living things.

George Edwards published his four-volume work, *A Natural History of Birds . . .* , in 1743–51. The basic penguin was described, based on a specimen given to Edwards by a Mr Peter Collinson.

The mysteries of the penguin remained unexplained; for example, the feathers were more like 'scales of serpents'. Although Edwards knew that penguins came from the Cape of Good Hope and from the Straits of Magellan, he was not prepared to nominate a 'Native place' for the birds.[10] Geographically, penguins were still from distant unknown places.

Newspaper editors and writers included descriptions of penguins in reports of travels and voyages to exotic lands. These

A realistic attempt at depicting Magellanic penguins or Blackfooted penguins by George Edwards in *A Natural History of Birds* (1743–51).

Latham's Fairy penguins, now known as Little penguins, from John Latham's *A General Synopsis of Birds* (1781–1801). Latham noted the New Zealand Maori killed them with sticks and ate them, considering them a delicacy.

accounts added a more popular conception of the bird to that circulated within circles of natural historians, readers of published travel books and sailors' conversations. Popular understandings of the use and attributes of penguins were established, and confirmed through a process of circulation and repetition. On Friday, 26 October 1744, the *Penny London Post* published a 'Continuation of a Voyage to the South Seas, under the Command of Commodore Anson'. In March 1741 Anson's ships were anchored off Penguin Island, where the crews saw many penguins and seals. Anson, like many voyagers before him, had read previous descriptions of the regions through which they sailed and knew what to expect. His story borrowed from earlier accounts: 'we find the Penguin exactly to answer Sir John Narborough's Description; therefore we beg Leave to give it to the Reader in that excellent Navigator's own Words'. Anson then quoted the famous passage from Narborough's late seventeenth-century story.[11]

In Europe, classification of the natural world into orders or classes was an important process of natural historians as they attempted to place the newly found animals and plants into a manageable framework. The first scientific description of a penguin appeared in the tenth edition of Linnaeus' *Systema Naturae*, in 1758. That honour went to the South African jackass penguin. Linnaeus named this species *Spheniscus demersus*.

The French first established a settlement at Port Louis on the Falkland Islands (Iles Malouines) in 1734. Penguin eggs had been an important part of settler diet up to the twentieth century. In 1766 Captain Louis Antoine de Bougainville sailed in *La Boudeuse* to explore the seas around Tierra del Fuego. On the way he stopped at the Falkland Islands and left us with a lengthy

Olivier van Noort's map of 1599 showing Penguin Island in the Magellan Straits.

description of the king penguin, adding further information and interpretation to that previously known. In the European imagination, penguins were gaining in sophistication and, consequently, in qualities:

> The penguin of the first class [of classification] is fond of solitude and retired places. It has a peculiar noble and magnificent appearance, having an easy gait, a long neck when singing or crying, a longer and more elegant bill than the second sort, the back of a more bluish cast, the belly of a dazzling white, and a kind of palantine or necklace of a bright yellow, which comes down on both sides of the head, as a boundary between the blue and the white, and joins on the belly. We hoped to be able to bring one of them over to Europe. It was easily tamed so far as to follow and know the person that had the care of feeding it: flesh, fish and bread, were its food; but we perceived that this food was not sufficient and that it absorbed the fatness of the bird; accordingly, when the bird was grown lean to a certain degree, it died.[12]

Thomas Pennant summed up current knowledge of the penguin in the Royal Society's *Philosophical Transactions* in 1768. He noted the characters of the genus 'Pinguins', listing the Patagonian penguin (king penguin from the Falklands), the lesser 'Pinguin' and the 'red-footed Pinguin'. Pennant closed his paper with the following comment: 'Lest the bird known, by the name of Penguin, in the northern parts of Europe and America, should be confounded with these, it may be observed, that it is of another genus; and it is by the later ornithologists very justly ranked with the Auks.'[13]

Scientific and popular European knowledge of the penguin

Ptenglonice
Aptenodytes patagonica Forster

J. Webber

remained tied to territorial expansion and sailors' observations. Knowledge of penguin habitat locations extended to the far south of the known continents in the southern hemisphere: Africa and South America. The British navigator James Cook was to change this, making extraordinary contributions to the understanding of the south. In particular, he made two remarkable journeys, forever dispelling the theories of a large southern continent. His voyages, undoubtedly territorial, also had scientific motives, one of which was the reconnaissance of the wild life of the regions through which he travelled.

On the first voyage (1768–71) with the *Endeavour*, and the second (1772–5) with the *Resolution* and the *Adventure*, Cook had with him naturalists who observed and collected the birds. On 7 January 1769, to the west of the Falkland Islands, Joseph Banks, then a young man with a keen mind and a passion for natural history, made notes about the penguins he saw. The Magellanic penguins were 'easily known by streaks upon their faces and their remarkably shrill cry different from any bird I am acquainted with'. Later, in New Zealand, he reported:

> The sea coast . . . has also a few of the birds calld by Sr Jno Narbourough Penguins, which are truly what the French call *Nuance*, between birds and fishes, as their feathers especialy on their wings differ but little from Scales; and their wings themselves, which they use only in diving and by no means in atempting to fly or even accelerate their motion on the surface of the water . . . might thence almost as properly be calld fins.[14]

During the second voyage, the astronomer William Wales saw penguins as the ships passed south of Penguin Island (Robben Island) off southern Africa. Later, on 26 December 1772, he noted that the crew drew them close to the ship's side by 'so happily' imitating their call. This was probably not the first time that crews had played with penguins, but it remains one of the first references to this form of contact.[15] On 30 December 1772, in latitude 59°23' s, longitude 170°1' e, Lieutenant Charles Clerke wrote in his log: 'the meeting with penguins has ever

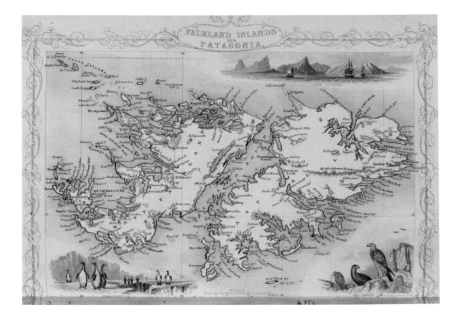

King penguins south of West Falkland on John Tallis's two-part map, *Falkland Islands and Patagonia* (1851).

been suppos'd a sign of the vicinity of some land but we've met with so many and are still at a loss for the least bit of Earth'. On the same day, Cook recorded: 'Hauled to the Northward for an Island of Ice, thinking if there were any loose pieces about it to take some on board to convert into fresh water . . . saw upon it about 90 penguins. We fired two 4 pound Shott at them . . . but they seemed quite undisturbed.'[16]

After calling at the Cape of Good Hope, Cook sailed westwards to New Zealand. On 31 March 1773 a shore party took specimens of little blue penguins from Dusky Bay; these were the first New Zealand penguins to be described scientifically – by Johan Forster, who named them *Eudyptula minor*. About the same time Tobias Furneaux of the *Adventure* reached Bruney Island, Tasmania, and also found little blue penguins.

58

Cook's voyages south heralded a change in perceptions of the penguin. Previously, penguin sightings had been seen as the sign of nearby land – a form of geographical and navigational certainty. Now found living in near-freezing seas, comfortable on icebergs and seemingly thriving in frozen wastelands, the penguin became an even more marginal and curious bird. On 29 December 1772 Wales wrote:

> On the Weather Side [of a large iceberg] . . . we were much surprised to find it covered with the Dung of Birds,

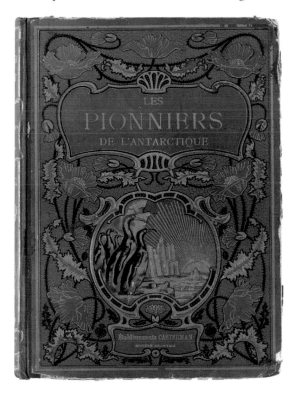

Elegant penguins face the sun, watchful inhabitants of a continent on the verge of human occupation. Cover of Yves de La Troplinière's *Au Pôle Sud: Les Pionniers de L'Antarctique*.

but were much more so when we opened the Seaside to it almost covered with Penguins. The great Numbers of these Birds which we had seen for some Days past made us hope that Land was near; but this circumstance in some measure damped our Expectations as it should seem from hence that they make these Huge Islands their principle Abode. It was thought that they might even breed here; but this seems however not probable, as the heat necessary to hatch the Eggs would melt the Ice where they lay and thereby defeat the very purpose it was intended to effect.[17]

The voyage continued, penetrating as far south as latitude 71°10' s. Blocked by thick pack ice, and with the appearance of icy mountains in the distance, Cook turned back, surmising correctly that the ice extended as far as the pole, and returned to New Zealand. From here, refreshed, the crew of *Resolution* set sail for Cape Horn, running east along latitude 55° s. They reached Staten Island, off the tip of Tierra del Fuego, at the end of 1774. Robert Cooper, First Lieutenant of the *Resolution*, wrote laconically in his log for 2 January 1775: 'Today boil'd shags and Penguins in the Coppers for the Ships Company's Dinner.' What did they taste like? On board the *Resolution*, sea birds were obviously an important item on the menu. Joseph Gilbert, the master, wrote: 'Hoisted in the Launch, having got from the Sea Lyons puncheons of blubber and four boatloads of penguins and shags which are exceedingly good eating.' But Lieutenant Clerke commented: 'The people are tired of eating Penguins and Young Shags, they prefer Salt Beef and Pork to either.'[18]

A natural historian, J. R. Forster, described an encounter with Rockhopper penguins, called 'Jumping Jacks' by the Falkland Islanders. While penguins may appear childlike, encounters with colonies were not considered peaceful outings, however entertaining they might be. Rockhoppers were acquiring a reputation for aggression and hardiness:

> They sleep very sound, for Dr Sparrman met one of them, which he kicked several yards by accidentally stumbling over it, without breaking its sleep, till by repeatedly shaking the bird, it awoke. When the whole flock was beset, they all became very bold at once, and ran violently at us, biting our legs, or any part of our clothes. They are excessively hard-lived, for having left a great number of them, seemingly dead on the field of battle, and going in pursuit of the rest, they all at once got up, and walked off with great gravity.[19]

Knowledge of the penguin entered the public domain in the late eighteenth century through travellers' accounts, natural history descriptions and reports in magazines and newspapers. These publications placed the penguin in the imaginative embrace of a wider public than sailors. While basically descriptive, they contained references to attributes and characteristics that were later to form part of the stereotypal penguin. On 17 January 1775 Cook's expedition reached South Georgia, which they took possession of in the name of George III. They found large numbers of King penguins, which they described as 'so dull as hardly to waddle from us'. The men ran up to the penguins and 'knocked them down with sticks'.[20] That year, as Cook was returning to Britain with his news of the south and its wild life, William Frederick Martyn published his *Natural History*, which included a summary of three species of penguin, the Magellanic, the 'black footed' of Cape of Good Hope and the northern (that is, the Great Auk). Although his work contained some reasonable information about penguins, it maintained an amusing tone in its comments about the bird's shape and attributes that continued the tradition of comic, extraordinary ways of description. Penguins, according to Martyn, were 'unwieldy' when on land:

> The duck is not half so unwieldy an animal as the whole tribe of the Penguin kind. They seem, when sitting, or attempting to walk, like a dog which has been taught to sit up, or to move in a minuet: their short legs drive their bodies in progression from side to side; and were they not assisted by their wings they would scarcely move faster than a tortoise.

He continued:

> These birds walk erect with their heads on high, their fin-like wings appearing as arms; so that when viewed at a distance, they resemble so many children in white aprons. From hence they are said to unite in themselves the qualities of men, fowls and fishes: like men they are erect; like fowls, they are feathered; and like fishes they have instruments resembling fins, which beat the water before, and answer the purposes of swimming rather than 'flying'.[21]

And in November 1775 William Clayton read a paper to the Royal Society on the Falkland Islands. According to his report in *The Times*:

> I consider the penguins as amphibious animals, partaking of the nature of birds, beasts, and fishes. There are four

kinds; the yellow, or king penguin; the red; the black or holey, from their burrowing under ground; and the jumping jacks, from their motion. These creatures, generally live in the sea, have very short wings, which serve for fins, are covered with very short thick feathers, and swim at an amazing rate. On shore they walk quite erect with a waddling motion, like a rickety child; and their breasts and bodies before being quite white, at a distance have, at first sight, the look of a child waddling along with a bib and apron on. They come on shore to lay and hatch their eggs in October: the yolks of the yellow, the holey, and jumping penguins are yellow; but of the red penguins it is red. All their eggs are good nourishing food, and a great refreshment to the seaman; but

Early mariners in the South Seas 'knocking them down with sticks'.

the flesh of these animals is coarse fishy, and wholly unfit to eat.[22]

The practice of indiscriminate killing of large numbers of birds could not be sustained without permanent depletion of population sizes. Several people noticed this in the late eighteenth century, including those in close contact with the damaged populations. A Newfoundland trader, George Cartwright, visited Funk Island, a home of great auks, in July 1785. He noted in his diary that the locals regularly took the eggs of the 'innumerable flocks of sea birds that breed there every summer'. He was shocked at the extent of the killing and predicted: 'If a stop is not soon put to that practice, the whole breed will be diminished to almost nothing, particularly the penguins: for this is now the only island they have left to breed upon: all others lying so near to the shores of Newfoundland they are continually robbed.'[23]

On Cook's and similar voyages, new wildlife was discovered, including new species of penguins. The penguins were taking on their roles as the entertainers of the wild, but they retained the attributes of inhabitants of a remote, forbidding territory – biological signposts at the edge of human experience and endeavour. Cook's news of the wealth of life on the far southern islands that he visited was followed, however, by a wave of men hunting seals for fur and elephant seals for oil. The coats of fur seals were becoming very popular in Europe, China and North America. The fur seals of the south were to be exploited so thoroughly that they were completely cleared out from some southern islands and driven close to extinction. By 1791 there were 102 vessels engaged in sealing in the southern ocean. British sealing expeditions reached South Georgia in 1778 and the United States fleets followed soon afterwards. In less than 50 years sealers

The Great Auk at Home, an oil painting by J. G. Keulemans (1842–1912), an idyllic setting without predatory sailors.

took 1,200,000 fur seals and 20,000 tons of sea elephant oil for the London market alone. Less than 100 years later the fur seals had disappeared from South Georgia. The commercial drive to exploit the riches of these new territories brought people further into the habitats of the most exotic penguins of them all.

3 Sealers and Zoo Collectors

Penguins became a familiar part of the life of the many sealers who flocked south to exploit the enormous numbers of fur seals. On remote islands on the way south, and then on islands close to the Antarctic continent, they established temporary camps and pursued their trade. Penguins provided food and in some cases warmth, since their fat-filled carcasses were used as fuel. As sealers lived in remote, forbidding, confusing territory, so penguins took on the attributes of the inhabitants of such a place: they became even more the symbols of life at the edge of human experience and endeavour. The proximity of these men (and some women) to concentrations of penguins inevitably led to increased familiarity and an enhanced understanding of the birds. The sealers were not sentimental about killing them for food or fuel, but the fascination of Europeans for the penguins' 'character' continued, under closer observation.

Sailors and collectors had previously tried to bring penguins back from their colonies, for collections and as pets. Penguins were not good travellers, however, and they were very hard to keep alive. Accounts noted that they went off their food (or 'sulked') and became thin before dying. Many still tried. In 1810 an island south-west of New Zealand was discovered by sealer Frederick Hasselborough. Macquarie Island teemed with wildlife, including fur seals, elephant seals and four species of penguins. It quickly attracted sealers once the richness of the island became known. The Macquarie Island penguins received wider notice as early as January 1816, when a story of royal penguins was published in the *Sydney Gazette*. The writer noted that the royal penguin appeared to be one of 'those species that cannot endure captivity, and every effort made in the Colony [New South Wales] to preserve alive such as have occasionally been brought from the Islands frequented by our sealers has proved abortive'. The survival rate was related to treatment and relative ignorance, however well meaning. In November 1815 a pair of royal penguins had been brought back to Sydney from Macquarie Island. One died shortly after capture, but the other was force-fed and occasionally placed in saltwater for a swim, with a piece of string tied around its leg. The bird lost its crest and lost weight, finally dying in January 1816. The article in the *Sydney Gazette* described the bird in detail.

> The oeconomy of the penguin is utterly unknown, and is likely to remain so until persons stationed upon the islands they abound in shall take the trouble to examine into its mode of living, and oblige the world with the natural history of a creature combining in its extraordinary nature the properties of the coarse amphibious animal, the bird, and fish . . . As we cannot preserve them alive, it is a pity they should be taken from their own shores to die a death of famine: to man they are an inoffensive brood, and do not deserve the rigorous treatment we inflict upon them by removal, when it is certain they cannot be kept alive by any mode of treatment whatever.[1]

Articles and stories such as these were no longer merely descriptive; they added a sympathetic, almost affectionate concern for the species and the impact of human beings on the natural world. Despite European discovery in the sixteenth century, Tristan da Cunha was not occupied until 1816, when a British garrison landed on the island. Although the troops left the following year, Corporal William Glass chose to remain behind, and established a tiny settlement, together with his wife. As the small community grew it developed a unique relationship with the northern Rockhopper (Macaroni) penguin. Essentially, the penguin was seen (and in some ways remains) as an economic resource for the isolated islanders, who now rely on government support, tourism and their own hard work for a living. Over the years the islanders collected penguins (and other seabirds), and used the bird for oil, its feathers for bedding and sometimes penguin scalps for rugs, hats and purses for trade. In season, rockhoppers were heavy and fat, but their flesh was fishy and was not usually eaten. The eggs, however, were harvested regularly.

The British artist Augustus Earle found himself stranded on Tristan de Cunha in March 1824. At that time there were six permanent adult inhabitants and several children. He subsequently described his eight-month stay in a letter to a Hobart newspaper, and published a lengthier account in 1832. His engrossing story included descriptions of his encounters with Rockhopper penguins. On first sight, he wrote, 'their extraordinary appearance startled me . . . from the head, just over the eyes, is placed a bunch of bright yellow feathers, hanging down on each side of the face, which gives the animal an animated and beautiful appearance: it is from these fantastic feathers they receive the name Macaroni'. In September Earle visited a penguin rookery by boat to collect eggs. It was extremely noisy and distracting –

a common characteristic of penguin rookeries at breeding time. The penguins were on the beach and their nests stretched far up into the long tussock grass on the hillside. Because a surf was running, Earle and one other swam ashore from the boats with bags around their necks.

As our business lay with the noisy part of this community, we quietly crept under the grass, and commenced our plundering search, though there needed none, so profuse was the quantity. The scene altogether well merits a better description than I can give – thousands, and hundreds of thousands, of these little two-legged erect monsters hopping around us, with voices very much resembling in tone that of the human; all opened their throats together: so thickly clustered in groups that it was almost impossible to place the foot without dispatching one of them. The shape of the animal, their curious motions, and their most extraordinary voices, made me fancy myself in a kingdom of pigmies. The regularity of their manners, their all sitting in exact rows, resembling more the order of a camp than a rookery of noisy birds, delighted me. These creatures did not move away on our approach, but only increased their noise, so we were obliged to displace them forcibly from their nests; and this ejectment was not produced without a considerable struggle on their parts; and, being armed with a formidable beak, it soon became a scene of desperate warfare. We had to take particular care to protect our hands and legs from their attacks: and for this purpose each one had provided himself with a short stout club. The noise they continued to make during our ramble through their territories the sailors said was, 'Cover 'em up, cover 'em up.'

And, however incredible it may appear, it is nevertheless true, that I heard those words so distinctly repeated, and by such various tones of voices, that several times I started, and expected to see one of the men at my elbow . . . Each one lays three eggs, and after a time, when the young are strong enough to undertake the journey, they go to sea, and are not again seen till the ensuing spring. Their city is deserted of its numerous inhabitants, and quietness reigns till nature prompts their return . . . After raising a tremendous tumult in this numerous colony, and sustaining continued combat, we came off victorious, making capture of about a thousand eggs, resembling in size, colour, and transparency of shell, those of a duck; and the taking possession of this immense quantity did not occupy more than one hour, which may serve to prove the incalculable number of birds collected together . . . but the whole of those we took turned out good, and had a particularly fine and delicate flavour. It was a work of considerable difficulty to get our booty safe into the boat – so frail a cargo – with so tremendous a surf running against us. However, we finally succeeded, though not without smashing a considerable number of the eggs.[2]

After publication, Earle's story became widely known. His graphic description of the visit to the penguin colony was described like a military raid. It was considered exciting enough for republication in an anthology of adventure stories, *The Book of Enterprise & Adventure*; *Being an Excitement to Reading for Young People*, which was published in London in 1851. Penguin stories were becoming popular and even exciting, as well as feeding a desire for tales from exotic parts of the world.

Meanwhile, penguins living in Antarctica or on Antarctic islands came to the notice of Europeans. These birds initially fell into the same descriptive patterns as their known family members. They were the source of food, entertainment and comfort. More significantly for the story of penguins, human perceptions of penguins received a new twist. In some tales they were seen as small humanoid inhabitants of a remote, hostile and confusing land.

One of the first of the sealers to work in the far south was Captain Edmund Fanning. His home port was New York and his ships the *Betsey* and the *Aspasia*. A considerate and observant captain, Fanning took the time to describe the Rockhopper penguins he saw on the Falkland Islands. His experience was similar to that of Cook some years before (and no doubt to that of the Falkland Islanders, who worked the rookeries for a living). The colony was noisy, crowded and hard work. The penguins, so close together that they had to be pushed and kicked away, were very aggressive, and pecked his blood. Fanning described the penguins and their behaviour, noting their energetic leaps from the sea and the threats from predators:

The Mackaronie is about sixteen inches high, and has on each side of its head a tuft of thin feathers, richly variegated in colour, which gives the bird a very consequential and proud appearance. In its walk, or rather march, it is as erect as a soldier. One could sit for hours, and observe their manner of approaching the shore, after a spell of feeding in the sea; to effect this purpose, they make choice of a spot where the sea breaks directly against the side of the rocks and while yet some seventy yards from the landing place swimming moderately along in solid columns of hundreds together, toward it, commence diving and coming up again to the surface at short distances; this is continued until about within thirty feet of landing, when they dive again, and come up in the surf ten or twelve feet from the rock, with such velocity as to land upon it perfectly erect, and clear of the surf; immediately forming an Indian file, and divided into distinct bodies, each division having its own leader, whom they follow, proceeding in their march up the valley or chasm, to the rookery, apparently with as much conceit of their superiority in point of discipline as ever a company of soldiers manifested on a public parade. The gratification derived from beholding a scene like this, is in a great measure counter balanced, in the destruction committed among them by the sea-lions, which place themselves a few rods from the landing place, in the water, watching the time that the penguins are about to commence diving to land, at which period they are the most compact. At this moment, the lion settles himself under water with the intention of swimming under them, and when a suitable opportunity offers, rises

Macquarie Island's Rockhopper penguins, cheeky, inquisitive and territorial.

suddenly in their midst, and seizes one or more of the birds in his jaws; then raising part of his ponderous body out of the water, he bites and shakes this, his prey, until they are torn to pieces, then devouring them.[3]

The gruesome killing of the penguin by the sea lion must have been an extraordinary sight. The plucky, defenceless bird was literally torn apart by its predator, reminding us that penguins are victims in the relentless struggle for survival in the far south. Such confrontations, particularly with the leopard seal as predator, still hold observers riveted in horror. It has now become a cliché of southern wildlife films, but with no loss of impact.

William Smith discovered the South Shetlands, off the Antarctic Peninsula, in February 1819, after being blown towards the islands while attempting to round the Horn. On a return voyage the following year, the men landed on the islands, finding immense quantities of penguins (and fur seals). On 22 January 1820 the crew of the *Williams* landed on New South Britain, amid the 'intolerable stench' of guano from a nearby penguin colony. Claiming this land for Britain was an imperative, and the men strode ashore, looking also for water and fur seals. They found both, but the penguins were so thick on the beach that they had 'to cut a lane through them'.[4] Soon after, sealers reached the South Shetlands. In a devastating series of seasons lasting until 1823, most of the fur seals were exterminated. On the South Shetlands alone, 320,000 seals were slaughtered. The sealing gangs quickly became familiar with the local penguins. A sealing captain, Robert Fildes, was shipwrecked on the islands and wrote an account of his experiences, calling the penguins 'half form'd birds'. In 1821 he established a rudimentary campsite on Cora's Island in the South Shetlands. The men set up a tent, 'the grand part of which', Fildes wrote,

Penguins at Home.

consisted of 4 lines of puncheons in a square . . . one of these . . . was taken possession of by the cat and two penguins one day came up out of the water and took up their stations alongside of her in the cask they never minding the people in the tent or the cat, nor the cat them . . . shipwrecked puss used to sit purring alongside . . . apparently comfortable and pleasd with their company. These penguins used to go to sea for hours and as soon as they landed again would make direct for the tent and get into the cask. The crew would sometimes plague them and endeavour to keep them out . . . but they always found a way to get in by getting under the canvas.[5]

In 1834 Charles Darwin was in the Falklands on the *Beagle*. In his log of March 1834 he noted the determination that was becoming a common reference to penguin behaviour. Darwin placed himself between a penguin and the water:

75

It was a brave bird; and till reaching the sea, it regularly fought and drove me backwards. Nothing less than heavy blows would have stopped him: every inch he gained he firmly kept, standing close before me erect and determined. When thus opposed he continually rolled his head from side to side, in a very odd manner, as if the power of distinct vision lay only in the anterior and basal part of each eye.[6]

In the early and mid-nineteenth century great national expeditions circled the globe, with territorial, commercial and scientific aims. These expeditions encountered penguins – including those of the far south – and their reports, both private and public and within the scientific community, continued the flow of information about penguins to the public.

In 1839 the French navigator Jules-Sébastian-César Dumont d'Urville sailed from France with the ships *Astrolabe* and *La Zélée* on a voyage around the world. They sailed south to Antarctica, landing on what was called Adélie Land, after Dumont d'Urville's wife. There he found the small black and white penguin that he named the Adélie penguin. In January 1840 the ships were near the coast of Antarctica, and on 20 January they landed on a small island. The crew 'hurled down the penguins, who were much astonished to find themselves so brutally dispossessed of the island, of which they were the inhabitants'. The men collected everything of interest for natural history that they could gather. The penguins were 'living trophies' of the conquest – an interesting comment. The idea of penguins as the 'inhabitants' of Antarctica became a standard description of the birds as the human occupation of the continent continued.[7]

Also in 1839 Captain James Clark Ross set off to make a series of magnetic observations in high southern latitudes for the

British Association for the Advancement of Science. With HMS *Erebus* and HMS *Terror*, he reached Hobart, Tasmania, in August 1840. Ross determined to penetrate further south. By January 1842, in latitude 66° s and longitude 156° w, *Erebus* and *Terror* were drifting in the pack, searching for a way through the ice. On the ice floes were parties of emperor penguins. Unused to human contact, they appeared to be 'stupid' and to allow the men 'so near as to strike them on the head'. Ross's men collected specimens of these 'wonderful creatures' for science. The bodies were preserved in casks of pickle for the physiologist and comparative anatomist at home, who dissected some and found from 1 to 4.5 kg (2–10 lb) weight of pebbles in their stomachs. A quick analysis of these identified granite, quartz, vesicular lava, scoriae and pumice.[8] One of the unresolved questions of the time about the south concerned the nature of the continent itself. Was it rock or simply a vast body of ice? The discovery of rocks and pebbles inside a penguin's stomach was an intriguing sign of the continent's true nature.

Another aspect of the Emperor penguin emerged from this period of Antarctic discovery. Lieutenant William Reynolds, a member of the United States Exploring Expedition on the *Peacock*, wrote in 1840 about an Emperor penguin that was collected for science: it was a 'mammoth penguin' and 'a beautiful and kingly bird'.[9] The perception of the Emperor penguin as something noteworthy in the natural world, with a sense of nobility, was developed throughout the following years, to reach an almost mythical status in the twenty-first century.

Despite the difficulties of transportation and of keeping penguins, some survived the journey back to Europe, taking their places among both zoological and natural history collections. In zoos penguins performed an entertaining, attractive role and acted as inducements to visit. In 1865 the first penguin to be

The first penguin exhibited at London Zoo in 1865 attracted much interest. Ernest Griset painted this watercolour celebrating the apparent calm of the bird amid the excitement.

exhibited in London was displayed at the Zoological Gardens in Regent's Park. It was the star attraction of that Easter Monday, during which 23,069 people visited the zoo. *The Times* reported on the bird, pointing out its curious features and movements, thus linking it to popular perceptions.

This animal is singularly misshapen. It stands upright, with a stolid and ridiculous air of gravity. Its head and tail lie in a perpendicular and not a horizontal line. Its wings, which have no feathers, hang down by its sides like two shrivelled arms. A traveller, speaking of these birds, says that their erect attitude and bluish black contrasted with their white bellies might cause them at a distance to be taken for young children with white bibs, and no one who sees the bird now at the gardens will fail to appreciate the description. Nothing could be more grotesque than the slow and awkward motions of the animal as, with its dumpy body it hobbled yesterday on its short legs round its enclosure after the keeper, who held out a fish to it. This is the first of these animals which has been brought to this country from the southern hemisphere . . . A sight of this penguin alone will well repay a visit to the exhibition.[10]

During the last quarter of the nineteenth century a diversity of stories and descriptions of penguins and their behaviour was published in books and newspapers. Most of these focused on the peculiarity of the birds, although many were affectionate. The spread of these stories was also a means of classifying the penguin in the popular imagination, defusing the different, exotic nature of the bird and welcoming it into our understanding and control. The syndication of items describing penguin behaviour was a certain sign of the popularity of penguin tales. The spread of these stories confirmed and

Penguin Island in the Crozet group, Southern Ocean, a remote and forbidding land that on occasion provided shelter and food, including penguins, for shipwrecked sailors.

demonstrated their roles as peculiar birds, sometimes comic, but somehow different. An item first published in the *New York Times* and then, across the globe in the New Zealand *West Coast Times* in 1877, made a humorous point of the report that survivors of the wreck of the *Strathmore*, on the Crozet Islands in 1876, were forced to live mainly from penguin eggs. The survivors' complexions grew 'clear and fair' and then their hair 'assumed a gorgeous golden tint'. According to the story, the cause was the presence of 'sulphuretted hydrogen' in the penguins' eggs.[11]

Published in 1873, W. L. Buller's *Birds of New Zealand* is a classic in ornithology, and Buller's descriptions and stories have become part of New Zealand's scientific folklore. In the section on penguins, Buller fantasizes about the fate of the Little Blue penguin, many of which die in fierce storms off the New Zealand coast. Buller's penguins are a romantic part of another world. There is a nobility in their death.

> I found [their bodies] particularly abundant on the open beach at Waeteku, in the exact spot where in 1864, HMS *Harrier* pitched a shell into the retreating body of Ngatiporou warriors, killing their chief, Poihipi, with several of his followers, whose bodies were afterwards buried in the sand-hills near the spot where they fell. The encroachment of the sea has exposed the bodies of these unfortunate braves, and they are now tossed about with the ebb and flow of the tide, just as remorselessly as the bodies of the Little Penguins – victims of the pitiless storm and rolling surf.[12]

Buller's references to penguin included many affectionate and humorous stories. According to him, the crested penguins

Yellow crowned (Yellow eyed) and black penguins, in Walter Buller's *Birds of New Zealand* (1873), an example of the increasing accuracy of scientific knowledge and illustration of these birds.

could be made pets, but they too eventually sulked and died unless released. However, he told the story of 'Major Mair's' crested penguin that would come up regularly at feeding time and would make its wants known by a loud chuckle accompanied by a comical twisting of its neck. It also had a habit of waddling off to a 'duck-gang', a distance of a quarter of a mile, apparently for company, and then coming back at the usual time to be fed.[13]

The capture of penguins continued, often with interesting results and accounts. In 1875 the New Zealand government purchased the yacht *Hinemoa*. For the next 69 years it worked its way around the New Zealand islands and the Pacific pursuing a variety of purposes, including the collection of natural history specimens. Often penguins were transported on the *Hinemoa*. One story was told by Buller to the members of the New Zealand Institute. Captain Fairchild would keep penguins on deck, in enclosures according to species. On one occasion, one of the Rockhopper penguins stood on a slightly higher part of the enclosure than the others and 'vociferated loudly', while the others kept quiet 'and appeared to listen'. Fairchild built a small 'pulpit', and watched as one of the penguins 'like a member of the French Senate . . . addressed his fellows until ejected by another', who climbed onto the pulpit and had its 'turn'. Throughout the 'address' the penguin audience remained 'quiet and orderly'.

From time to time, Buller had a private collection of penguins that he turned loose into his one-acre garden. Here they became subjects for observation and story, and a form of semi-domesticated pet. The Rockhoppers would 'scuttle' away into the shrubbery, 'and when fairly out of sight one of them indulged in vociferous chatter for some time, as if addressing his fellows and proposing some plan for their mutual safety'. A Snares Island penguin, initially aggressive, became tame and 'docile', persistently following the gardener around to be fed. This particular penguin lived in a kennel with a Gordon setter. 'He lived in terms of perfect amity with the dog, for whom at times he testified his affection by gently pecking him all over with his bill, an attention which the sagacious animal seemed quite to appreciate.'[14]

Perhaps the story of the penguin and Walter Haybittle was published in the New Zealand *West Coast Times* as an oddity, but it now reads almost as an antidote to the sometimes cloying sentiment that later grew around penguin tales. Captain Fairchild gave a penguin to Haybittle as a gift for his child, but on the way home in a horse-drawn cab a fight between the penguin and its new owner flared. After much grappling, the 'remorseless' penguin 'cuffed' Haybittle with his flippers and then bit him firmly and fiercely on the nose, reducing it to a swollen and bloody mess. After rescuing Haybittle from the 'triumphant' penguin, the bird was quickly released to an unknown fate.[15]

The stories contain mostly warm and comforting references to penguins and their interactions with people. The more materialistic role of the penguin – as economic or scientific resource – continued, however. On the Falkland Islands egg collecting went on and many birds were rendered down for oil. Others saw more commercial opportunities. In 1880–81

THE EGG-CART.

In season, sealers on remote southern islands gathered penguin eggs in large numbers to supplement their meagre supplies.

83

a merchant from Bluff in New Zealand, Walter Henderson, started a trade in penguin skins, most of which were turned into fashionable hand-warming muffs for ladies. Crested penguins were obtained mainly from the colonies at the Antipodes and Snares Islands off New Zealand. By the time the trade stopped, having become unprofitable, Henderson had purchased more than 15,000 skins from men working on the islands. The Dunedin business of Elder & Co. had pioneered the sea elephant oiling industry on Macquarie Island from 1878 to 1884. Later, Joseph Hatch started his oil industry there with a gang killing sea-elephant bulls in 1887, but in 1889, with fewer bulls and the Norwegian development of a steam pressure digester that could extract oil from smaller animals like penguins, Hatch realized the potential of the millions of penguins on the island. Oiling plants were eventually established at Lusitania Bay, South East Bay, the Nuggets, Hasselborough Bay and Bauer Bay.

Throughout the nineteenth century, concerns about the impact of civilization on the natural world were expressed. Earlier, in the eighteenth century, concerns about the destruction of economic resources had been voiced in relation to sealing and the survival of the auks. The predictions of people like George Cartwright were confirmed on 4 June 1844, when the Icelanders Sigudur Islefsson, Ketil Kentilsson and Jon Brandsson set out on a hunt and killed the last two Great Auks in existence.

Such attitudes were eloquently and passionately exposed in *The Dictionary of Birds*, published in 1893, under the heading Extermination:

Extermination, literally a driving out of bounds or banishment, is a process which, intentionally or not, has been and still is being carried on in regard to many more species of Birds than most people . . . seem to recognize, and one that has frequently led to the Extinction . . . of the species affected. The inhabitants of islands are especially subject to this fate. In them each species has long been brought into harmony with its circumstances, and relations with its fellow-creatures have so far become mutually adjusted that in the long run the balance between them is preserved, and the stock of each remains the same one year with another. But the appearance on the scene of man, and especially of civilized man, upsets the equilibrium. Even if he do not immediately begin to bring the virgin soil under cultivation by felling the primaeval forest or burning the brushwood, he almost always introduces certain animals which make war on the aboriginal population – directly in the case of Cats and Rats, indirectly in that of Goats and Rabbits, or both ways in that of Hogs. Against such enemies, whether forcibly attacking them or insidiously robbing them of food, the most part of the indigenous species are unprepared and absolutely helpless. In the majority of instances each of the islands so colonised has its own peculiar fauna, and its ancient inhabitants with difficulty preserve their existence, or wholly succumb.[16]

The *Dictionary* writers focused their concern on specific instances and condemned the wholesale killing of penguins in rookeries, most notably in the Falkland Islands, where owing to the 'ravages of man' numbers had been greatly reduced:

Incapable of escape by flight, they are able to make enough resistance or retaliation (for they bite hard when they get the chance) to excite the wrath of their murderers, and this only brings upon them greater destruction, so that the interest of nearly all the numerous rookeries is spoilt by the disgusting details of the brutal havoc perpetrated upon them.[17]

The *Dictionary* authors were suitably horrified by a story concerning the Johnny or Gentoo penguin of Macquarie Island, which was

rapidly decreasing in numbers, owing to the destruction to which it is subjected at its breeding-places. It is disgusting to read (*Phil. Trans.*, vol. 168, p. 155) that on the occasion of the observation of *Venus* in 1874–5 on Kerguelen Land, where this species had many settlements, a naturalist should have to write of one of them – 'The whole of this community of Penguins was subsequently boiled down into 'hare soup' for the officers of HMS *Volage*. It is obvious that officers of this kind should not be sent on scientific expeditions.'[18]

By the late nineteenth century penguins had established their role as entertainers in zoos, and the press enthusiastically took up the news. More formal arrangements for keeping penguins were also part of a growing public appreciation. On 13 October 1888 the London magazine *The Graphic* noted that in the Zoological Society's gardens at Regent's Park, specimens of Rockhopper penguins from New Zealand were kept in the fish house, which was well supplied with

water and artificial rockwork, so that the peculiar actions of the birds in both elements can be observed. At feeding time a large glass-fronted water tank also enables visitors to watch and admire the rapid flight through the water in pursuit of the fish with which it has been previously stocked. The crowds that daily assemble here at the hour when this performance takes place testifies to the fact that it is one of the sights of the zoo.

A year later, the *Manchester Times* published a description of Belle Vue Gardens, where penguins, 'among the funniest objects to be found' in the gardens, were trained

> to perform a number of tricks such as running races and walking up and down stairs , the prizes being fish, which the winner swallows without any ceremony whatsoever. They also go through a ridiculous burlesque of a Rugby scrimmage which may last an indefinite time, unless one of the birds is fortunate enough to secure one end of the fish, when the latter will disappear to the apparent great astonishment of the other birds.[19]

The penguin came to symbolize or represent many human needs, as entertainer, as economic resource and as a symbol of outrage for a growing number of people concerned about what we now call human impacts on the environment. By the end of the nineteenth century, penguins were playing out roles as economic resources in the popular press. The authors of these tales also hinted at the value of the birds in providing a moral guidance. 'Uncle Old Man' of the Children's Hour of the *Manchester Times* serialized a children's adventure story called 'Crozet Joe'. Joe and the capable Mrs Harwood and some children were marooned on an island in the southern ocean. With the energy and kindness of Mrs Harwood and the skills of Crozet Joe, the small group managed to survive quite well in a cave.

They used local resources for food and fuel: giant cabbages, seals and seabirds. Penguins featured in this tale of survival. Once established in a cave, called 'The Refuge', Crozet Joe is determined to take eggs from the nearby penguin colony. The penguins were aggressive and Joe had to remove them forcibly from their nests and in doing so was attacked: 'Very soon . . . he began to tumble them over unceremoniously with his feet.' He collected eggs in his pockets, leaving the dirty ones. While doing so he accidentally trod on a penguin chick. 'The little one was badly wounded, and Joe reflected that it would be kinder to at once put it out of its misery rather than leave it to a lingering death.' Joe kept the chick's body for food and returned to The Refuge. There Mrs Harwood fully appreciated the importance of the discovery of the eggs, and realized that the penguins 'suggested resources not hitherto thought of'. An experienced traveller in the south, she thought that the seabirds of the island could provide 'light and warmth' and asked Joe to get a bigger bird.

'I don't like killing things but . . .', said Joe.
Mrs H. insisted, 'But we must kill things if we are to live . . .'
'You shall have a big bird in a brace of shakes.'

Joe left the refuge and returned with a 'full grown' penguin, the fat of which was transferred to the lamp. Water was boiled over the small fire of the lamp and eggs placed in the water. '"Aren't we toffs with boiled eggs for breakfast" said Joe. "We'll have just as many as we can eat. There's plenty for fetching, and the fowl house is not far away."'[20]

'Crozet Joe' is written in the classic children's story format of the time. Central characters include a kind, capable and organizing mother figure paired with a resourceful and supplying father. There are just enough threats to thrill, but a warm central

'home' with plenty of food to comfort. The penguins do not have human characters, but their role as food and fuel was by now time-honoured. In this story we have the added function of penguin as an inadvertent player in the story of life. They must be killed (as by implication other animals must be killed) to survive. This is the natural order of things.

Creche of Emperor penguin chicks, Cape Washington, Antarctica.

In stories about their contacts with people, penguins took on more than the straightforward characterizations of animals in the wild. Accounts of the birds took on more subtle meanings. The characters assumed an allegorical role – similar to those in fables. They began to convey messages, not just of life's lessons but of other aspects of the human relationship with the world. It was a role that was to become more pronounced in later years. In places of environmental extremes, penguins were companions as well as message bearers or curiosities, creatures enabling a sort of solace, perhaps even sanity. In 1893, on the eve of the first push of people onto the Antarctic continent, W. G. Burn Murdoch wrote of his men working on the peninsula: 'the men say they are the only things worth coming to see in the Antarctic, and no matter how melancholy a man may feel, if he sees one of these jolly little fellows he cheers up.'[21]

4 Antarctica to Animation

By the late nineteenth century, the Antarctic mainland remained as the last great territorial prize for geographers and explorers. The way south was known as a remarkable journey through regions of natural wonder and danger, marked by exotic icescapes and creatures. The penguin was a noted inhabitant of these places. The first sight of them was a significant experience for the southern visitor. A source of location, entertainment and nutrition, the penguin was marked on maps and in expedition records as illustration, observed as science, coddled and bullied as entertainment and eaten as survival. With no vegetation or human marks of occupation, such as buildings and roads, and with the sense of the normal scale of things broken by enormous ice walls and glaciers, a sense of unreality was created, enhanced by cold, dry air and long silences. In this, penguins presented a very strange sight indeed. The fact that these birds seemed to survive readily, almost easily, only added to the sense of unreality. Where the barren and strange wilderness fostered a craving for human society, people often described penguins and penguin behaviour as if they too were human. Penguin rookeries were described as cities, penguin groups as a committee or gang. It is as though this mode of expression was fulfilling a need for human contact.

In these conditions, it was at times difficult to distinguish penguins from humans. The crew of the *Belgica*, trapped in the ice in 1898, thought that a group of penguins on the winter horizon was a visiting mission and hurriedly got dressed. Roald Amundsen was sent out to investigate. It was the same in 1950 when a group of surveyors was lost on the coasts of South Georgia. At first, rescuers on board a ship thought that the waving arms signalling need for assistance belonged to penguins.

Two species feature in Antarctic stories – the Adélie, the 'clown' of the Antarctic, and the Emperor penguin, the stoic, diplomat and model of endurance. Stories and films about travels to see these birds, to study them and their life cycle took on the tone and forms of modern epics. The accounts of the first visitors forged the comic characterization of the Adélie penguin. Between 1903 and 1910 Louis Gain, who made two trips south with Jean Baptiste-Charcot, wrote the first scientific accounts of the Adélie penguins. He too was captivated by their appeal:

> On beaches accessible to the rookeries, there is usually a
> host of birds gathered there by the thousand, reminding

Used as research subjects and for food, penguins were sometimes also the butt of amusing jokes . . .

me of the throngs of human beings that are attracted on fine summer days to our great beaches in France. They chat little; simply a few reflections whispered in a low tone, while in the distance one hears the stir of the noisy city . . . what confusion in these cities of the Adélie; how many quarrels over stolen pebbles and property rights; how many battles too, started by jealous husbands! And all this occurs on ground wet with melting snow, stained with mud the colour of wine dregs.[1]

Edward Wilson of the British National Expeditions led by Robert Falcon Scott was a very keen ornithologist, and his delight with the penguins serves as an example of the many times that scientific observers have broken into anthropomorphic descriptions. In 1901 the expedition vessel *Discovery* was approaching the Antarctic, travelling through closely packed ice floes. It was a great opportunity to observe the ice birds. Wilson was a happy man. He watched as the Adélie penguins came towards the ship, gazing at the visitors and crying in wonder:

> [one] pokes his head constantly forward on this side and on that, to try and make out something of the new strange sight, crying aloud to his friends in his amazement, and exhibiting the most amusing indecision between his desire for further investigation and doubt as to the wisdom and propriety of closer contact with so huge a beast.[2]

Lieutenants Skelton and Royds were the first to locate an emperor penguin colony at Cape Crozier, in 1902. Visiting the colony was a difficult and arduous exercise. They scrambled their way through icefields, chunks of ice and cold before coming upon a few penguins. Wilson wrote a long report about them, the results of four seasons' visits and assessments. His report is scientific writing, not given to passion or romance, but there is still an element of quest – both geographical and scientific – in the publication. Cape Crozier, for example, is described as 'a focus for wind and storm, where every breath is converted, by the configuration of Mounts Erebus and Terror, into a regular drifting blizzard full of snow'.[3] And the birds were found in a place where 'The ice cliffs used for shelter are so much undermined and so unstable from the pressure of the Barrier up against Cape Crozier that no man in his senses would camp for a single night beneath them. Yet these birds huddle for upwards of five months of every year persistently.' The men were impressed

with the beauty of the emperor penguin, which Wilson noted was the 'largest and handsomest of penguins'. Soon after emerging from the darkness of a southern winter, they saw a group of fifteen. These must have seemed a revelation and were later described by the artist Wilson:

Emperor penguins at Cape Crozier, Ross Island, sketched by Edward Wilson while on expedition.

> Always full of curiosity, they would stand around in a group making comments to one another about our appearance. . . . Such a group formed an exceedingly beautiful picture; their lemon yellow breasts shone like satin in the sun, and their bluish backs and jet-black heads set off the golden yellow patch on the side of the

neck, and the rose or lilac streak on the lower bill. The back and breast, if the bird had just been in the water, would glitter with crystals of ice and salt.[4]

Wilson and the others were beginning the research into a remarkable bird. The facts of its life and reproductive cycle were gradually understood. The ice-bound reproduction cycle, now so often evoked as an act of stoic endurance and worthy of awe

A leopard seal chasing Emperor penguins, Edward Wilson's depiction of the theme of the defenceless penguin versus a remorseless predator.

Wilson, a zoologist and bird lover, painted these heads of Emperor penguins, which were first published in the expedition publication *South Polar Times*.

EMPERORS
YOUNG &
OLD.

and admiration, was then a puzzling series of scarcely credible actions, those of an 'eccentric' bird:

> We now, however, knew a good many of the habits of this bird, and they are eccentric to a degree rarely met with even in Ornithology. First, in choosing the darkest months of the Antarctic winter in which to incubate its eggs, which are laid probably in the first week of July. Then, not only in the choice of season for its nesting, but of place. It must needs lay its single egg upon sea-ice with no pretence at nesting, removing the egg at once from the surface of the ice to rest upon its own feet. There it holds it wedged in between the legs closely pressed to a patch of bare skin in the lower abdomen, and covered from exposure to the cold by a loose falling lappet of abdominal skin and feathers.[5]

The reproductive cycle, the fierce parental instincts, the enduring quality of the emperor's life were becoming part of the scientific and common understanding. The story of the reproductive cycle has become a central theme of the modern interpretation of the bird, standing in common imagination as a natural marvel. Among other suggestions about the bird, it was seen as an ancient relic, the most primitive of birds, and therefore one of great interest. Wilson's work and the respect with which he asked questions and wrote his conclusions have helped set the ways in which we now see the Emperor penguin. Wilson noted many aspects of the bird, but one sentence stands out as a motive for later action: 'The possibility that we have in the Emperor penguin the nearest approach to a primitive form not only of a penguin, but of a bird, makes the future working out of its embryology a matter of the greatest possible importance.'[6]

As humans' experience of penguins increased and as information about them wound into the increasing volume and diversity of penguin stories and impressions that developed in the nineteenth century, ideas of the birds grew increasingly fanciful. They developed attributes and roles that became more divorced from the realities of the bird and its habitat. People would still engage with penguins, but within the forms of communication about to be developed the clichés and descriptions took on new lives.

The concern about birds expressed by the editors of *A Dictionary of Birds* carried on into the twentieth century. When Wilson and others visited Macquarie Island in 1901 on the way south, they saw the killing of penguins there. Back in England, Wilson campaigned against the cruelty. The growing public affection for the penguin and the anthropomorphic ways of describing it made it easier to elicit sympathy and organize a campaign. The popular image of penguins was gathering a new, political, potency. Wilson spoke to people and groups, including the Society for the Protection of Birds. His concern and that of others spread. On 1 June 1905 an article entitled 'The Destruction of Penguins' was published in the New Zealand newspaper *Otago Daily Times*. The journalist attempted to rouse public opinion in order to halt the 'shameful' trade in penguin oil, referring to Wilson's campaign and noting also that the increased human presence in the south opened up more breeding grounds for exploitation. He appealed to the public using the perceived harmlessness, unusualness and 'ancient nobility' of the birds:

> The unfortunate penguins have always been treated, whenever their breeding places were visited, with exceptional brutality . . . With the example of Steller's sea cow and the great auk before us . . . it is intolerable that the whole world should be robbed of yet another of its heritages to afford a temporary satisfaction to the greed of a few individuals. In order to be effectual no time should be lost if the world is not to be rendered the poorer by the loss of at least some members of this most remarkable family of birds.[7]

In literature, penguins continued to be used as exemplars or models for moral guidance. In 1908 the French writer Anatole France wrote a satire on human nature by depicting the transformation of penguins into humans. France makes it clear that his penguins were auks, but they have many similarities to the southern penguins. In *Penguin Island*, morals, customs and laws are satirized within the context of the fictional land of Penguinia, where the animals were baptized erroneously by the myopic Abbot Maël. The abbot first mistook the penguins for

L'Ile des Pingouins.

people and believed that the Lord had sent him to teach them
the divine law. Touched by their gravity, silence and tranquil
deportment, Maël likened the birds to the 'senate of a judicious
republic' or to the 'Fathers of Athens disputing on the benches
of the Aeropagus', adding: 'Your hearts are pure and your hands
are innocent, and the truth will easily enter into your souls.' The

penguins perceived a reassuring gentleness in the monk and answered the old man. 'And their voices were soft, for it was the season of their love.' Still believing the birds to be people, Maël taught the penguins about baptism, and about 'Adoption, New Birth, Regeneration, Illumination'.[8]

Primarily a satire, and clearly written with tongue in cheek, France's story is amusing. But it is also a charming analogy for the accommodation of penguins into the human imagination as 'good souls'. Deluded perhaps, but accepted in trust and affection and bestowing a certain moral authority. As wild animals they were good, innocent; as humans evil. As soon as the penguins were transformed into humans, they began robbing and murdering each other. On one level, the book is a satire on France's political history, including the Dreyfus Affair. On another, it is ultimately concerned with the perfectibility of mankind.

Adélie penguins at a colony.

Diving Emperor
penguin.

In the Ross Sea region on the eve of the First World War, one of the great journeys of modern exploration was undertaken. A moving, exciting and extremely popular account of the trip was first published in 1922. The *Worst Journey in the World* has been republished many times since and remains as one of the most emblematic journeys of Antarctic history. It has been described as 'the weirdest bird-nesting expedition that has been or ever will be'.[9] The 'quest' involved the scientific (almost quixotic) search for Emperor penguin eggs by Apsley Cherry-Garrard, Edward Wilson and 'Birdie' Bowers while members of the British Antarctic Expedition (1911–13).

In the first winter of this expedition, the three men left the comforts of the Cape Evans hut five days after the Antarctic mid-winter celebrations on a 67 mile (108 km) trip to the Emperor penguin colony at Cape Crozier. The emperor, then described as the most primitive bird in existence, wintered in the blizzards of Antarctica. Scientists, Wilson included, believed that the foetus of the Emperor penguin would reveal information about the evolution of the penguin. 'We travelled for Science', wrote Apsley Cherry-Garrard – perhaps with a healthy dose of dramatic emphasis by George Bernard Shaw, who helped him write the book.[10] To find the eggs with embryos, the men were forced to travel in the Antarctic winter, a hazardous, almost foolhardy enterprise, battling (for once the cliché is true) extremes of cold and wind to reach the colony at Cape Crozier.

After dragging themselves through the bitter weather for nineteen days, the men heard the penguins before they saw them, the cries cutting through the Antarctic air. The birds were still a day's march away. When they were a few miles from the colony, the men stopped and built a small stone hut at the foot of Mount Terror. Soon afterwards they were the first to see a colony of emperor penguins in winter. They gathered eggs from the birds, killing three for skins and for the blubber, which they used for the stove. With three eggs – precious evidence considering the trials of retrieval – the three bedded down for the night. A ferocious storm blew up and ripped the canvas hut roof to shreds. The men lay exposed to the elements. After a terrifying night during which they feared for their lives, they gathered their belongings and courage and turned back. It was a frightful and dangerous time. They reached the Cape Evans hut to be greeted 'as beings from another world'. The story has become a classic of Antarctic adventure. Although the main characters are human, and heroes, the emperor penguins play their part as ciphers of the unknown, as a silent chorus.

On his return to London Apsley Cherry-Garrard took the eggs to the Natural History Museum to present them to the curator. He was greeted with the words: 'Who are you? . . . this ain't an egg shop'. When finally he met a man of 'scientific aspect' he was rudely dismissed. 'You needn't wait', he was told. But Cherry-Garrard waited for a receipt – a measure of his respect for his companions, by now known to have died with Robert Scott on the return journey from the South Pole. The eggs were examined and found to be no different from any other birds' eggs, and therefore containing no further knowledge of evolution. Cherry-Garrard later wrote that he made the trip 'in order that the world . . . may build on what it knows and not on what it thinks . . . If you march your Winter Journeys you will have your reward, so long as all you want is a penguin's egg.'[11] In an intriguing footnote to the story and incident, staff of the Natural History Museum displayed the emperor penguin eggs at a seminar of heritage conservators in 2007. The fact that the objects were the internationally renowned Emperor penguin eggs made the display even more dramatic. The display was part ritual – the showing of heritage relics – part publicity and part atonement. Or so one participant thought, until museum staff began to make excuses rather than apologize for their counterparts' earlier behaviour towards Cherry-Garrard.

The Antarctic penguin has expanded our notion of penguin considerably. In some expeditions, it seems that discussion and comment led to the penguins being seen as an alternative,

Eastern Rockhopper penguins, French Antarctic Territory stamp, 2008.

Tristan da Cunha one penny stamp.

diminutive human community. Penguins became more than anthropomorphic. They have become vehicles for the expression of our hopes, fears and humours. At their extreme, such descriptions of penguin behaviour are examples and lessons for humans. Apsley Cherry-Garrard claimed that:

> All the world loves a penguin: I think it is because in many respects they are like ourselves, and in some respects what we should like to be. Had we but half their physical courage none could stand against us. Had we a hundredth part of their maternal instinct we should have to kill our children by the thousand . . . [12]

He went on:

> The life of an Adélie penguin is one of the most unchristian and successful in the world. The penguin which went in for being a true believer would never stand the ghost of a chance. Watch them go bathe . . . What they really do is to try and persuade a companion of weaker mind to plunge: failing this, they hastily pass a conscription act and push him over. And then – bang, helter-skelter, in go all the rest.[13]

Argentine stamp, 1987.

Falkland Islands stamp.

British Antarctic Territory stamp, 1997.

The men were learning of the extraordinary life of the emperor penguin:

> The Adélie penguin has a hard life: the Emperor penguin a horrible one. Why not kill off the unfit right away, before they have had time to breed, almost before they have had time to eat? Life is a stern business in any case: why pretend that it is anything else? Or that any but the best can survive at all? And in consequence, I challenge you to find a more jolly, happy, healthy lot of old gentlemen in the world. We must admire them: if only because they are so much nicer than ourselves! But it is grim: Nature is an unforgiving nurse.[14]

The leap from sea onto ice is a popular moment in both film and still photography.

The rapidly developing technology of film brought new perspectives onto the evolving penguin character type. The Antarctic

photographers Herbert G. Ponting and Frank Hurley both filmed the wildlife of the Antarctic with still and moving picture cameras. Ponting, and perhaps more importantly his leader Scott, was aware of the 'great potential and educational and moral value of the kinematograph film of the adventure . . . Wilson could not only tell about the zoology of the Far South, but by means of photographs and films he would be able to show the nature of the animal'.[15] Frank Hurley, whose film of the Australasian Antarctic Expedition of 1911–14 was distributed around the world, wrote that 'nature study' was 'by far the most interesting work' in Antarctica. 'Those quaint old Penguins and Seals help pass away much weary time, and many pleasant hours [were spent] in the rookeries studying their human-like antics'.[16]

Both Ponting's film *90° South*, released in 1914, and Hurley's film, later given the title *Home of the Blizzard*, were silent. They were among the first nature films distributed and were early forms of documentary. As such, they stand as hallmarks in cinema history. The footage was shown to audiences keen to see examples of the new entertainment technology and images of an almost completely unknown land. Although familiar with earlier nature films, and primed by movies of the hunt or chase in remote parts of the world, these movies of the south were of the battle between man and nature, and one of the characters was the penguin. They appeared in these films not only as examples of the wildlife, but also as plucky and fearless, as entertainers, sometimes as clowns. The penguins, particularly the Adélie penguin, became popularized as a vaudeville character.

In the United States Lee Keedick promoted Hurley's film zealously. Posters announcing the footage and accompanying lecture declared that 'Sir Douglas Mawson's Marvellous Bird, Animal and Travel Motion Pictures' were a 'pictorial account of

over: Drawing of a penguin by the explorer Sir Ernest Shackleton.

the achievements of the Australasian Antarctic Expedition, Showing Animal, Bird and Deep Sea Life, Raging Blizzards, Mountainous Seas and Towering Ice Bergs of the Frozen South'. If this was not enough to entice a sizable audience, the posters reprinted enthusiastic reviews. The *New York Times* noted that 'the camera's record of Sir Douglas Mawson's journey into the Antarctic has more entertainment in it than a hundred archive photo pages, and each individual penguin is more amusing even than those gymnastic movie comedies wherein everyone of the actors falls down at fewest seven times'. The *New York Mail* was just as enthusiastic: 'Screamingly funny. The penguins are supreme comedians.' To reinforce the point the poster also noted: 'The penguin is more humorous than the monkey – and a million of these were found in one Rookery and photographed. The penguin is the originator of the famous Charlie Chaplin walk.'[17] Not true according to Chaplin, who in an interview in 1916 denied that his shuffling walk was derived from that of a penguin, but from an old drunk he had watched while in England as a child. Once the comparison had been made, however, it stuck, and the relationship between Chaplin and penguins has remained as a testament to them both.[18] The penguins in Hurley's footage struck a chord with audiences around the world. In 1915 the *Toronto World* published a review, noting that 'when the lecturer called attention to their funny waddling gait, which he likened to the famous Charlie Chaplin walk, several hundred school-children in the audience roared their approval'.[19]

Photography of wild animals in the south was a planned activity. Scenes and 'acts' were constructed when they did not occur naturally. Ponting noted that his work was made 'just as any drama film is produced . . . various characters concerned would have to be made to play their parts'. On one occasion, Ponting's patience grew thin after waiting in vain for the drama

previous: Emperor penguins, often described as courtly and diplomatic inhabitants of the ice.

of a skua raid on a penguin's nest to occur naturally. The penguin was taken from its nest and tied up while the camera focused on the empty nest. Eventually the skua, 'the pirate' of the story,

> pounced upon the egg and carried it off; and I had the incident recorded on the film. . . . the owner then was released, and its return to its pillaged home was also recorded; also, its concern over the loss, and its final 'it can't be helped' attitude and expression, as it settled down on the bare stones with resignation.

The production ended with an act of reconciliation. Ponting took two eggs from other nests and placed them on the nest.[20]

Soon after the return of the men from Scott's and Mawson's expedition, the First World War began and a seemingly insatiable demand for fats and oils developed. The killing and rendering of penguins on Macquarie Island shocked many, including the well-known Antarctic explorers Douglas Mawson, Frank Hurley and Apsley Cherry-Garrard. Both Hurley and Mawson had seen the trade on Macquarie Island during their visit in 1911, while members of the Australasian Antarctic Expedition, and they retained their horror at the practice. After the war people began to speak out against it. Like Wilson before the war, Mawson addressed scientific societies, such as the Royal Geographical Society. Hurley addressed the public through the Australian press. 'I can only term the destruction there as grim tragedy, the remembrance of which makes me shudder still', he wrote to the editor of the *Sydney Morning Herald*. Sparing no detail in the attempt to influence the reader, he added:

> The penguins round a corner, full of curiosity and that is the last of them; for a knock on the head and a kick sends

them into the boiler. It is one of the most pitiful sights I have ever witnessed . . . when the boiler is full the lid is sealed down and the steam turned on. This wanton butchery takes a toll of some 150,000 annually.[21]

There was an international movement to seize the public's attention. Campaigners contrasted the charm and harmlessness of the penguin to the cruelty of the killing of such a creature. By 1919 the world was weary of war and brutality, and remained shocked at the intensity and scale of the destruction. Although stunned at the immensity of the war's effect, the reading public remained susceptible to appeals using propaganda, such as the reported German atrocities in Belgium during the early stages of the war. At the beginning of April 1919 Cherry-Garrard wrote to *The Times* explaining that the stories from Macquarie Island 'make the atrocities of Belgium sound like a Sunday school treat'. He continued: 'The penguin has won a little bit of affection from all of us because he is entirely lovable, and because he snaps his flippers at the worst conditions in the world. If we do not help him now we can never look him straight in the eyes again. Poor penguins, but poorer we.'[22] That same year he also wrote an article for the London *Spectator*, appealing for government control over the killing of Antarctic fauna. After listing measures that should be taken to safeguard southern species, he concluded: 'Otherwise the penguins will call us Huns, and we shall deserve every bit of it.'[23] The reference may have struck a chord, it was repeated in a letter to *The Times*. On this occasion he also thanked H. G. Wells:

A chilly penguin delivering an important wartime message.

'there are some Huns among them', the penguins say, 'but the nice people, like *The Times* and Mr Wells, and others not so well known (but just as nice) have been too

much for them' . . . when the frost is in the trees and the snow is on the ground you will hear them [the penguins] say 'thank you', as does yours sincerely, Apsley Cherry Garrard.[24]

The widely read and influential author H. G Wells published *The Undying Fire* in 1919. Through his main character, Wells examines the cruelties of the natural world. The happiness of animals, Wells's narrator reflects, 'is at best like a transitory smile on a grim and inhuman countenance'. He considers the lives of king penguins:

You will have seen pictures and photographs of penguins. . . . They express a quaint and jolly gravity, an aldermanic contentment. But to me now the mere thought of a penguin raises a vision of distress. I will tell you . . . One of my old boys came to me a year or so ago on his return from a South Polar expedition; he told me the true story of these birds.

The narrator continued, outlining the daily life of the king penguin in dramatic and pessimistic terms before getting to the point:

But the king penguin draws near the end of its history. Let me tell you how its history is closing. Let me tell you of what is happening in the peaceful Southern Seas – now . . . These birds are being murdered wholesale for their oil. Parties of men land and club them on their nests, from which the poor silly things refuse to stir. The dead and stunned, the living and the dead together, are dragged away and thrust into iron crates to be boiled down for their oil. The broken living with the dead . . .

The people who run these operations, you see, have had a sound commercial training. They believe that when God gives us power he means us to use it, and that what is profitable is just.[25]

The penguins were now part of a popular tale of environmental destruction, characters in the drama of man's cruelty and carelessness of his impact upon the natural world. The campaign had its effect. The Australian prime minister withdrew the penguin hunter's licence in 1920, thereby bringing the practice to a halt.

A different penguin story, with a very different penguin character, also emerged from these times. In 1918 the Australian writer and artist Norman Lindsay published the children's story *The Magic Pudding*. Written as a reaction to the horrors of the First World War, the story of Bill Barnacle and Sam Sawnoff, 'the penguin bold', tells of their adventures trying to keep a self-replicating pudding (Albert) from the clutches of pudding thieves. All the characters, including Albert, are strongly drawn. Sam Sawnoff, a tall penguin possibly modelled on a King penguin, is a rough pugilistic first mate to Bill. Sam is not the simple food source of Crozet Joe, or the pitiable creature of H. G. Wells; he is no model for behaviour, but is a larrikin – lovable but prone to misdemeanour. He and Bill have killed: they rolled the previous owner of the pudding off an iceberg, for the cook would not share his food. There is a moral ambiguity to Sam that is at once out of type, and very appealing.[26]

In 1928 men of Richard Evelyn Byrd's first Antarctic expedition came south to establish the 'colony' of Little America. In late December the men and dogs landed at Discovery inlet, an ice bay in the giant Ross Ice Shelf. Groups of Emperor penguins came towards them. Paul Carter wrote the following, describing the Emperor penguins as 'Antarcticans':

From some distance off the expedition members saw a long file of slowly moving objects approaching. To [Paul Siple] they seemed like a procession of 'monks filing in reverence from a monastery'. Closer up they proved to be representatives of those First Citizens of Antarctica, the emperor penguins. Collectively ponderous and grave, while individually ridiculous . . . they stopped, clustered into a group, and put their heads together to discuss the situation. Then they turned as one to face the intruders, and one of the largest . . . stepped forward, clucking his approval.

Penguins in *Little America Times* (1935), a newsletter circulated to supporters of Rear-Admiral Richard E. Byrd's several Antarctic expeditions.

"*He used to be mascot of the Byrd Expedition!*

Very slowly he lowered his head upon his breast in a gracious bow, so low that his beak almost touched the snow, and delivered a long welcoming speech which lasted for several seconds and sounded like the clear blast of trumpets playing a range of several notes. Then very, very slowly he raised his head and looked at us . . . Seeing that we did not comprehend, he began to shake his head in disgust. A critical member of his delegation, who evidently thought his speech had not been properly presented, approached the chairman and nudging him to one side proceeded to deliver the welcoming speech himself, but to no avail. We humans were too ignorant of the penguin dialect to understand what was expected of us.[27]

Carter's Emperor penguins are of a type, the graceful diplomatic penguins, the rightful possessor of a new and strange land in which humans feel awkward and uneasy – out of place. Their performance is also described like a pantomime, and there was even more ridiculous behaviour to follow. In 1938, when the Nazis laid claim to portions of Antarctica, they landed and greeted one curious penguin with a 'Heil Hitler' salute, which as one shore expedition member afterwards admitted, 'did not make much of an impression'.[28]

In 1933 Macquarie Island was declared a wildlife sanctuary, and the penguins received full government protection. At about the same time Cherry Kearton and his wife sat down with African penguins, observing and writing about their experiences. A very popular book emerged: *The Island of Penguins* followed the format of popularizing the descriptions with a theatrical anthropomorphism. Penguins were not just childlike, comical, inoffensive, creatures; they were also little citizens of our planet. Their rookeries were small villages, the occupants familiar,

Jacqueline Reading's *Chilitoes*, published for children in the 1930s, is a world of inoffensive penguins living through everyday family problems.

non-threatening and entertaining neighbours. Kearton gave names to his penguins: 'Shylock, The Alderman (who dined excessively), The Magistrate, The Tramp, (a ragged, out-at-elbows creature), The Albino, and One-leg. . . . I met the proud and the meek, the bully, the mischief maker, the comfortable old gentleman, the despised weakling and the social outcast'.[29] He found the island

> crowded with small inhabitants with fashions, ways, and social institutions of their own; and during the months that I spent with them, I constantly found myself comparing them with people in the world from which I came . . . and sometimes . . . as happened when

Gulliver compared the Lilliputians to the people of eighteenth century England, the comparison was decidedly
in favour of the islanders.[30]

Like other authors and filmmakers Kearton exaggerated the
penguin's human-like characteristics to make his work more
accessible. The accounts and descriptions now read as simplistic.
His retelling of the reproductive cycle of the black-footed penguin
is described under the chapter heading 'Family Matters', and is
told in graphic terms of penguins meeting, squabbling, mating
and having chicks. In reality, these penguins arrive at a nesting
place, meet, find a burrow or dig one, mate, lay eggs, care for the
chicks and return to the sea. It is a harsh and competitive cycle,

with the need for burrows and the constant search for food determining the success of reproduction.

In *The Island of Penguins*, a pair of birds, the 'loving couples', set up house and lay eggs. If not a pair then courtship begins, a behaviour that involves an approach, which if successful ends in 'marriage'. The two birds kiss – Kearton means this literally:

> The beaks touch, and with necks outstretched and heads well up in the air, the birds rub their beaks against each other with a clicking noise. This lasts for ten or fifteen seconds; flippers are outstretched, and sometimes the husband in his ecstasy will embrace his wife all the time. That is the marriage ceremony.[31]

'House building' follows. 'Mr Penguin turns the first sod' and continues with 'Mrs Penguin' until the burrow is complete. It is 'furnished' with sticks, which are then the target for 'thieves', or worse, because sometimes another pair will occupy the burrow. If so, 'Mr Penguin sails into the attack. And pretty Mrs Penguin, not to be outdone, becomes a virago and follows her husband to the fray.' Once in repossession, our penguins 'do a great deal of lovemaking, becoming vastly sentimental in the process'. Eggs are laid and Mr P., a 'model of fatherhood', takes his turn in the hatching'. Two chicks eventually hatch and feeding begins, the adults taking turns to go out to the fishing grounds. About three months later the 'children' are fully fledged and learn the lessons of swimming and feeding – 'Young Master Penguin summons up all his courage and faces the waves.'[32]

While it is easy to criticize Kearton's sentimental style, he does provide the basic details of the life cycle and the book was very popular, going into many editions. It was also another chance for a concerned author to comment about the human impact on this 'beautiful, fascinating bird', then used as bait for cray-fishing. The South African government banned this use of penguins and Kearton commented: 'I wish all governments would show a similar interest in all the lives of wild creatures.'

Kearton (and presumably his wife) found distraction, comfort and entertainment in the careful and affectionate observations of their neighbours. He continued a scientific tradition – the close examination of the animals within which he found himself – and a sociological tradition: anthropomorphizing the penguins in an attempt to find amusement, companionship and the confirmation of purpose.[33]

During the first half of the twentieth century, in communities like that of Tristan da Cunha, economic necessity overrode other values. The local northern Rockhopper penguins were used for a range of purposes. In season, penguin eggs were taken by the thousand. The birds were eaten, when fat, and also boiled down for oil, which was used for various purposes, including, mixed with linseed oil, as a waterproof coating for canvas boats. In the early twentieth century 'tosselmats' were made to trade with the crews of passing ships. The mats were composed of 25 to 30, sometimes even 40 scalps, and the making of these articles required the killing of an equal number of adult birds. They were edged by the bright tossels of long yellow feathers that the penguins have over each eye. These small skins were sewn together in different ways. Most commonly, the mats were of a singular shape with the tossels radiating from the centre. There were 'single-row mats', with only one row of tossels, and double-row mats, which had an additional larger row of tossels outside the first row. But mats of rectangular shape were also made. The mats were decorated with coloured ribbons. A circular mat was decorated in its centre by a large rosette. Bright red silk ribbons were used. The Tristanites also made

Emperor penguin egg at Cape Washington.

hats, caps, purses and bags from penguin skins. The feathers of the birds were used for pillows and mattresses. The feathers were either gathered from the large mounds on the ground – found during and after the moult – or taken physically from the bird as it moulted.

In 1938 a group of Norwegian scientists stayed on Tristan da Cunha, visiting the nearby islands. Their story, *Tristan da Cunha: The Lonely Isle*, was published in 1940. Erling Christophersen wrote a lively account, describing the interactions and conflict of the colony with a literary relish – here is the angry penguin, symbol of nature's wildness, even ferocity. The colony of 'the world's worst-tempered penguin' grew in the mating season, August:

> battles . . . characterized by the blindest rage . . . [the rockhopper] stabs his enemy in the tender flesh with all the force his burning temperament can put into his thick beak (beaks are used for tugging, tussling and nipping with the most refined cruelty), pummels his back with steel hard flippers, and everywhere are groans, as eyes are put out and feathers fly. What a life![34]

While the chicks are growing, there is constant movement as the adults go to sea to feed and return. The penguin parade, a vital part of any colony description, is usually described in comical terms. Christophersen writes to type:

> When a penguin goes down to the sea, he is worth watching. Emerging into a clearing in the tussock grass he stands and takes his bearings of the sea, just as a drunken man sights at the nearest object he can grab hold of. On land the penguin hops as if competing in a sack-race, at the same time bending his neck up and down so that his golden fringe dangles in time with the hops. Every now and again he stumbles and rolls over piteously. Up he gets again and hops on, all in one movement, as if dignity had to be upheld at any price. Then he stops nervously and looks quickly round, so that his crest wobbles, in case anybody should have seen him.[35]

Anxious to reassure the reader that our penguin does not come to harm, Christophersen assures us that 'penguins seldom do themselves any injury in this way as they are well padded with fat and are round and soft, so that they always fall lightly'. He continues:

> But here we come to the surf. As soon as he is in his right element, a couple of rapid strokes with the flippers and he is off, to emerge, a few seconds later, sixty yards out. In frolicsome mood he leaps above the surface of the water, jumping in yard-long arcs through the air. After which he indulges in more material delights, fish and crayfish being his fare.[36]

On 24 March 1938 Christophersen, with two others, watched the herding of penguins on Stony Beach. It was a 'sight worth seeing':

> The penguins were gradually encircled, however, and the feathers of the much beset animals soon began to fly, whilst the sun gleamed on hundreds of nervous golden crests. Here and there one would roll out of the ranks and bounce like a ball. The hill ended in a precipice a few yards high, and here the throng was greatest, all being terrified of falling over the edge. The confined penguin masses at the edge became more and more restless, those on the outside trying hard not to be pushed over. But the pressure from behind steadily increased: at least a thousand penguins were encircled, and suddenly several hundred tumbled over the edge. A heavy avalanche of living, squirming birds slid down the side, whilst a gust of wind whirled the feathers into the air. Before I knew where I was, I suddenly found myself in the middle of a snow-storm of feathers which filled the air; clouds of sand and dust arose to complete the fantastic and grotesque

picture. Here and there penguins broke away from the flock in headlong flight, whilst the men rushed hither and thither as if insane, whistling and screaming to make the creatures run in the right direction.[37]

The capture and transportation of penguins continued in its particular fashion. The penguin, still described as a weird and friendly creature, now became an object of economic value – deserving of care. The curiosity value and relative ease of capture made penguins an ideal animal to take and house. Despite problems with keeping penguins, particularly those from further south, people continued to catch and attempt to hold them as pets, or as exhibits in zoos. Here they were popular, and in one case the unknowing inhabitants of architectural history.

In 1934 a modernist-styled, reinforced-concrete penguin enclosure, designed by Berthold Lubetkin, was opened at London Zoo. Designed with an element of fantasy, the Penguin Pool began what was later called 'a tradition of zoo architecture'. 'Antarctic' penguins lived in what became known as 'Berthold Lubetkin's Penguin Pool'.[38] Perversely, or perhaps as a result of one of those decisions made by zoo administrators due to space or popularity of creature, the pool was sited between the Lion House and the wolves' dens. From the administrators' point of view, the pool was to be hygienic to overcome some of the common problems of keeping penguins, and enough space was needed for the viewing public. Tanks, rocky space, nesting chambers and beaches made of rubber were provided, as well as two spiral pathways from the top of the enclosure to the water. A glass-sided tank was built to show the penguins swimming. With its combination of curved walkways, long pool and deep tank, the enclosure fostered displays of penguin behaviour that

London Zoo's award-winning Penguin Pool designed by architect Berthold Lubetkin in 1934, now an architectural heritage site rather than an animal enclosure.

audiences were most familiar with – 'their waddling gait and their grace and agility in the water'.[39]

The Penguin Pool became a popular attraction, as people came to see both the penguins and the breakthrough in architecture. In 1936 the popularity of the Penguin Pool and the success of its architecture were matters of public comment. One critic put it succinctly when he commented on the joint appeal, noting that the pool might not be described as architecture in the fullest sense, 'but rather a large object of abstract sculpture or a permanent stage setting'. He continued:

> But anyone who has seen the penguins performing their elaborate music-hall turns upon its inclined planes soon realizes that this is no objection: to provide a perfect setting for these incredible creatures, in the London Zoo with its enormous popular appeal was its essential functional problem.[40]

126

In 1970 the enclosure was listed as a building of special architectural interest. In 2004 the penguins were moved to a more suitable enclosure, but as a significant example of modernist architecture, the pool remains, and is visited by a different sort of audience. Critics of the old enclosure noted that it was unsuitable: in that it got too hot for the penguins, and 'boiled' them; that foxes easily got in and killed the birds, which could also fall from the curved walkways into shallow water and kill or injure themselves.

Capturing the southern penguins and bringing them back alive is a wildlife story with a difference. Richard Byrd's expedition was involved in bringing emperor penguins back from Antarctica to the zoo in Washington, DC. In 1947 two emperor penguins were seen watching a football game between the crews of two ships. The birds, which 'became rabid fans', were captured and held:

At first they refused to eat, but for about two weeks Mr Perkins spent hours every day stuffing frozen fish, in each

The new Penguin Pool at London Zoo.

127

In *Little America Times* (1935), President Teddy Roosevelt with his teddy bear welcome home Admiral Richard Byrd and his travelling bird from a second expedition to Antarctica.

of which was a multiple vitamin tablet, down their throats; finally the birds started to eat of their own accord and seemed reasonably contented. Curiously enough, they did not appear to suffer greatly while the ship was passing through the intensely hot days of the tropical Pacific.[41]

Thirteen Emperor penguins had been brought back to Washington in 1941 by Malcolm Davis, keeper of birds at the National Zoo, and they survived for seven years, kept in a specially built refrigerated cage.

Down in South Georgia in the 1950s penguins and penguin eggs were collected to provide food for the whalers who worked from the island during the summer. In 1955 H. K. Lillie was with a small group of men who rested after a collecting expedition and discussed 'the hurting of our small friends'. All members of the gang were fond of the penguins 'and we felt more than a little, just what thieves we were, taking advantage'. The conversation led Lillie to reflect that 'in our modern ideas of being clever with scientific inventions we have lost touch with life. We knew the price we as humans put on things, but rarely do we know the value of things themselves.' Lillie's book *Path through Penguin City* was immensely popular, spreading his fable of penguins and moral values to a wide international audience.[42]

Penguins continue to be the star exhibits in bird parks and zoos around the world. By the 1960s the problems of keeping them alive were being solved. Len Hill of Birdland in Bourton-on-the-Water, Gloucestershire, has six species of penguin at his bird park. King penguins were introduced in 1960 from South Georgia. The staff at Birdland have provided conditions as close as possible to the penguins' habitat and they seem to have survived and bred successfully. They are very popular, and hold a 'special place in his affections'. Birdland penguins provide entertainment and are a curiosity, although by then the exotic nature of penguins had worn off for most people. The scientific purpose

Emperor penguins as a symbol of Central Park Zoo, New York, on a souvenir mug, 2005.

of zoos and places like Birdland were explained in terms of protection. The penguins here would ensure species survival.

To maintain penguin supply, in 1970 Hill purchased two islands in the Falklands (Grand Jason and Little Jason) and became a 'penguin millionaire'. He later visited his islands, catching penguins to return to Birdland:

> I have been offered all sorts of fantastic sums, up to £50,000, to provide certain people with stocks of birds, but have only accepted commissions from those I know to be genuine conservationists who wish to preserve the species and breed from them rather than seeking to exploit the birds in any way. Often I make reciprocal arrangements with zoos throughout the world whereby I provide them with penguins say, and they give me a type of bird which hasn't previously been kept at Birdland.[43]

Almost as a contrast to the continuing relationship with 'real penguins' by traditional communities and researchers, versions of penguin in popular culture and media continued to diversify rapidly. Gladys the penguin starred in a British film of 1933, *To Brighton with a Bird*, also titled *To Brighton with Gladys*. A comedy

Penguin patterns have become a widespread form of decoration: a tea-towel design, 2008.

farce, the film featured the tribulations of a nephew in conveying a penguin to his wealthy uncle's seaside home. Penguin was moving from the wildlife subject, albeit with humorous commentary, to a deliberately crafted comedic role.

The widespread appeal of penguins, the familiarity of their body shape and colouring, and the ease with which images of them can be manipulated by animators to create accessible and attractive forms, led to penguin logos and trademarks. In 1932 the British manufacturer United Biscuits created the snack bar P-P-P-Penguin. Covered with milk chocolate and wrapped in foil, with an Emperor penguin on the wrapping, the biscuit became a popular treat. The concept of Willie the Kool penguin dates from 1932, when advertising executives decided to promote a menthol cigarette using a penguin as the central character. The advertising agency of Batten, Barton, Durstine & Osborn, Inc. developed the notion, and advertisements for KOOL cigarettes using the penguin were published for at least the next 25 years.

Penguin Books logo, the best-known penguin logo of them all, the first version of which appeared in 1935.

Dancing birds on the wrappers of Penguin bars, a chocolate-coated biscuit first introduced in Britain in 1932 by United Biscuits.

In 1935 Allen Lane released the first Penguin paperback. A logo designed by office worker Edward Young was inspired by the oddity and singular shape of the penguins at London Zoo. A new animated lineage for penguins grew. Both the biscuit penguin and Willie the KOOL penguin went through several redesigns. The idea was certainly popular and exploited. In the 1940s a pair of Willie the KOOL penguin salt and pepper shakers were available. By the late 1950s Willie had gone into decline, having lost much of his 'charm and appeal', according to one commentator. In the tough world of advertising, this is certain death.[44] The Penguin Books' logo has been updated several times and is now so popular and so recognizable that it is a commercially valuable product with its own website, and a six-second presence on YouTube.[45] The books are known simply as Penguins. They are adored, read and collected by many enthusiasts.

There are many twentieth-century literary references to penguins: they are oddities and observers, familiar, but conveying a sense of distance or strangeness. The novelist John Cowper Powys tired of disciples coming to visit, complained of them 'sitting like frozen penguins telling us with sleepy, grey tears of

lives and troubles'.[46] Later, in Henry Miller's famous novel *Sexus* (1962), people come to observe the character's lifestyle in a new apartment. They 'would waddle up to our room like auks and penguins and watch us in complete silence'.[47] Again, perhaps like a silent, critical chorus.

A classic of children's literature, *Mr Popper's Penguins* by Richard and Florence Atwater, was first published in 1938. House painter Mr Popper is sent several penguins from Antarctica. He and his wife put up the penguins at home and then train them to become stage stars before returning them to the wild – albeit the North Pole. The penguins are clown penguins, engaging but troublesome. The stories emerge from the different qualities of the penguins and the many escapades of the family as they cope with such strange 'pets'. The book remains on reading lists in schools in the USA, enshrining the popular perception of the birds as familiar clowns.[48]

On the other side of the world in South Australia, the poet and writer Max Harris and others began an artistic journal in

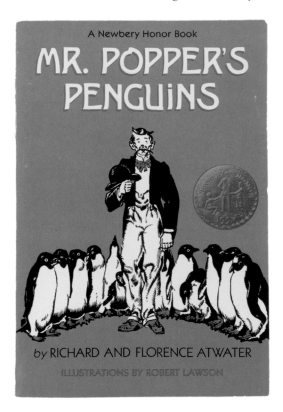

Book cover, *Mr Popper's Penguins* (1938) by Richard and Florence Atwater.

1940. *Angry Penguins* became a focus for writers and artists keen to foster a modernist and Australian approach to writing and painting. The journal and its adherents expressed what Harris called 'a noisy and aggressive revolutionary modernism' and represented a new language and a new painting of Australia. They were forthright and unapologetic, 'demanding' to be heard and seen. While the noise and posturing may be compared to penguins in a colony, the reference to angry penguins actually derives from a poem by Max Harris, *Mithridatum of Despair*, which includes the lines:

as drunks, the angry penguins of the night
straddling the cobbles of the square
tying their shoelaces by fogged lamplight.

The penguin is a strange but harmless oddity, out of place but non-threatening, a sign of sartorial splendour and literary angst.[49]

In December 1941 a famous penguin made his first appearance in *Detective Comic* number 58: Oswald Chesterfield Cobblepot. The artists Bob Kane and Bill Finger drew the Penguin as a twisted man who carries an umbrella because his father had died of pneumonia after a drenching in a storm. The story goes that the Batman Penguin was inspired by the 'huckstering waterfowl in a cigarette advertisement' (the KOOL penguin). The Penguin chose his dress as a gentleman to match the childhood nickname given to him by children, who commented on Cobblepot's hip ailment and love of birds. An intelligent criminal, the Penguin runs his affairs from the Iceberg nightclub. The character, absurd but recognizable from the odd shape, the waddle from the hip ailment and the affected formal wear, has become well known and continues to trouble Batman's quest for order. The Penguin

A solitary Emperor penguin will sometimes attend vessels at work in the sea ice.

took on new styles and characteristics as a star in the Batman TV series in the 1960s. With his swaggering, overdrawn TV performance, Burgess Meredith pushed the Penguin to further popularity. When Danny DeVito took the role in the 1992 movie *Batman Returns*, a darker Penguin emerged. It was still an attractive performance, but with a malicious tone that carried penguin representations into less affectionate territory.

The extraordinary growth of penguins in popular culture continued throughout the mid-twentieth century. In the United

States a penguin brand emerged from a chance outing. The story told about the choice of penguin has now become part of Munsingwear folklore, and is proudly displayed on their website. The Munsingwear penguin is a well-known clothing and merchandising brand. The sportswear line that was released in 1955 used a penguin as its logo.

Three employees were walking along a street in New York when they passed a taxidermist shop, in the display window of which were two penguins. The employees bought the penguins and on a flight to Los Angeles played with them. A fellow passenger suggested that they become the identity of the company. At a subsequent meeting, the sales team thought it was a 'fabulous idea'. 'It became so important in their minds' that two Pinkerton detectives were hired to 'come with their firearms to guard the penguins' while the team had lunch.

> No one knew (outside of the sales force) about the identity plan that we were working on with the penguin. [At] another meeting at the Leamington Hotel in Minneapolis, we put this little penguin on the conference table decorated with ribbons all around and flashing lights on

Danny DeVito in
Batman Returns
(1992).

a huge stage. We hired four off-duty policemen to guard this 'valuable bird' and to check the identity idea and told them what we were going to do with it. It was accepted with an excitement that you would not believe. . . . The future of Munsingwear sportswear began that year. Penguin has since become an American icon over the last 50 years.[50]

Animated penguins added a new troupe when Walt Disney studios released the film *Mary Poppins* in 1964. The penguins are depicted in what must by then have seemed like clichés – they are waiters, cheerful, obliging and witty. The production schedule for the film explains the introductions of the penguins. Bert, played by Dick Van Dyke, calls for a waiter:

A door in the background swings open and waddling out at high speed come four Penguins with napkins over their arms, dressed in waiter's garb, and water glasses and menus. To a wild musical SCHERZO, they settle around the table, brush off the crumbs, set down the water glasses, and one leaps onto the table, presenting Mary Poppins with the menu. The others poise themselves for the order.[51]

The penguins then perform a sand dance, accompanied by Van Dyke wearing a pair of impossibly long crotched trousers. He danced a waddle in these with his arms stiffly held at his side and hands extended sideways. The penguins were animated to match his dance. It may be viewed on YouTube at 'Penguin Dance Sing Along'.[52]

The film was enormously successful, not just because Dick Van Dyke danced with animated penguins, but because the story appealed to millions. It was a fantastic tale told to an audience increasingly used to animations, fantasy and image. With the developments of technology in the following decades and with a rapid social acceptance of the image, the role of the penguin was reproduced and manipulated in other forms.

5 Tourism, Films, Food

During the last three decades of the twentieth century significant changes in technology, tourism and social beliefs fostered new forms of penguin. As these representations evolved, penguins' role as entertainer, social indicator and moral guide continued, but with a life of their own. The extraordinary growth of the World Wide Web and the ease of communications led to new imaginative worlds for people and animals to populate. It is an intensely creative realm, one in which reality plays an inspirational but not a central part. Here penguins are a sympathetic symbol that has diversified so much in the human imagination that the results often bear little resemblance to the creature that exists in the wild.

Our contact with 'real' penguins, however, continues in many forms and stories. Scientific researchers spent time near penguin colonies, observing, analysing and gathering further information about the birds and their habitats and behaviour. This slow and careful accretion has enhanced a sense of the 'real' penguin, anchoring many into a more accurate view of the bird than the storms of digital representation and fantasy that now use a penguin character as a point of contact with an audience.

From the first ship-based tours of the 1970s, tourism to the far south and Antarctica has grown immensely. For the first time large numbers of well-informed and relatively wealthy people

The opportunity to see penguins in their thousands on the ice is a crucial aspect of the tourist experience in an exotic southern wilderness.

have witnessed and photographed the clamour and drama of penguin rookery life and seen the conditions in which penguins live and breed in their natural habitat. In the season 2007–8, nearly 30,000 tourists travelled by ship to Antarctica. The many species of penguin now feature on the relentless publicity of tour operators as real signs of the wilderness and adventure. Many of these visitors, now called 'adventure' or 'wilderness' tourists, remark on the unease or sense of intrusion they experience in the Antarctic wilderness. They respond quickly and affectionately to the penguins. It is reassuring to have cute and non-threatening inhabitants waving their flippers as if in welcome.

For nearly 200 years penguins have been used as examples or symbols of the state of the natural world. In the 1970s a broad social movement for change included more widespread discussions about these issues. They continue today, with penguins as symbols of human impact and of hope. Late in the twentieth century for example, the French decided to build an airstrip at their Antarctic base of Dumont d'Urville. The runway was to go through an Adélie penguin colony. Environmental groups were organized to pressure the French government to stop construction of the runway. The Adélie penguin and its rookery became a political symbol and an expression of the need for people to care for the wilderness and its inhabitants.

In 1987 the Australian writer and commentator Stephen Murray Smith visited the French base and saw the construction work. He was new to the continent:

Adélie penguin.

Then we anchor. There is the station helicopter ferrying construction materials down to the airstrip the French are building across the penguin rookeries, against many furious environmental protests. There, higher up on the snow slopes, we see for the first time the characteristic fawn colour of more penguin rookeries, snow and rock tinted by droppings. They are cheek-by-jowl with parked construction machinery and surveyors wandering around, our introduction to the insouciance of the Adélie penguins. . . . The penguins, in their native dignity and disdain, echo for us the message of the icebergs. I say to someone: 'There's something wrong in coming so far and finding people.'[1]

The penguins, inhabitants of a foreign world, seem to be forgiving of the human intrusion, and of the destruction around them. Here again are the symbols of good, almost pure penguins set against the encroachments of civilization. Ironically, the debate about the runway was finally resolved by an act of nature. A large wave swept over the small peninsula, destroying the work of the French engineers. No attempts were made to rebuild the facility.

Oil spillages from ships have damaged penguins for decades. In 2000 the black-footed penguins off South Africa were badly affected by an oil spill and many people joined together to ameliorate the damage. The iron-ore carrier *Treasure* was damaged off Cape Town and sank between Dassen Island and Robben Island – the Penguin Island of the first European voyagers. Some 13,000 tons of fuel leaked from the stricken vessel, 'oiling' 19,000 birds. After a mammoth effort tens of thousands of penguins were relocated. As oil continued to 'bubble out' from the wreck, penguins were boxed and removed by helicopter and boat, and then moved to safety by sheep truck; others were gently cleaned by volunteers. Penguins were tagged by scientists to keep a watch on them. Many of the penguins had survived earlier oil spills. It was an extraordinary, cooperative programme on the part of the people and organizations concerned. Images of oiled penguins and the efforts of concerned people ensured that publicity was maintained. A website was established to disseminate information about the rescue. This remains as an 'e-memorial' to the rescue.

The northern Rockhopper penguins of Tristan da Cunha are now a tourist attraction. Interestingly, they are still sought after as specimens, and in 2003 a plan to collect some of these birds from Nightingale Island by a South African animal collector and aquarium owner, John Visser, caused widespread concern. The scheme became the focus of an international campaign to protect the Rockhoppers, and by implication to continue to raise consciousness and to maintain the profiles of wildlife protectionist groups, such as BirdLife International. For all the right reasons, the penguin was again a symbol in an international effort to save wildlife. 'Once captured,' BirdLife International claimed, 'it is believed the penguins will be shipped to zoos and bird collections around the world on the unproven premise that the birds will be used to support captive-breeding programs.' The concern was shared by the Royal Society for the Protection of Birds and the European Association of Zoos and Aquaria.[2] Visser responded to the criticisms: 'I am a qualified zoologist and these penguins, which are treated excellently, go on to world-class zoos which have fantastic modern facilities. It is all part of an international captive-breeding program to improve the conservation of penguins, not reduce it.'[3] He sailed to Tristan and 'picked up' 240 penguins. As part of the deal he donated £25,000 to the island and defended his actions, noting

that the local population was estimated at 30,000 individuals. The penguins were transferred to zoos, including the Underwater World, Langkawi, a tropical resort island off the coast of Malaysia.

A penguin exploring the snow-dunes, Antarctica.

A Malaysian environmental group also condemned the trade. A spokesman for Sahabat Alam Malaysia said:

> What is inconceivable is that these penguins were plucked from the wild on Tristan da Cunha and transported thousands of miles to a place and land totally alien to their own

habitat. We are concerned about the stress during capture and transportation of these wild birds . . . it is doubtful whether all these birds will live to see a zoo visitor.[4]

A newspaper report, 'Walking with penguins' by Alan Teh Leam Seng, describes another, highly structured world. Here, the penguins were carefully protected. Before the author visited the penguins, he had to undertake a series of cleansings and wear special clothing to protect the penguins from potentially harmful micro-organisms. Once considered 'clean' the author and a keeper went through a large door into a 'freezer' and fed the penguins. When the birds had fed enough, 'they would slowly waddle away and dive into the pool for a truly relaxing swim. As I left the enclosure, I turned around for a last glimpse of the wonderful birds before the giant airtight door closed again.'[5] A measure of success of zoos and aquaria is the breeding rate of its inhabitants. Underwater World Langkawi has a total of 28 African penguins. Eleven eggs were laid in-house and the first one hatched on 17 March 2006. On 9 September 2007 the first rockhopper penguin chick was hatched.

Outside the care and attention of zoos and national parks, penguin pets are a novelty, given the difficulties of keeping them alive and the strictures of modern life. South American fishermen occasionally keep Humboldt penguins on their boats while they are at sea. There are reports of these birds being found well north of their range. In all likelihood the penguins escaped or were left by these vessels. It is possible to keep penguins domestically, as the Japanese owner of a king penguin demonstrates on YouTube. Their penguin, with backpack, leaves the house, waddles down a lane into a street and then into a store. Here the storekeeper puts goods into the backpack and gives fish to the penguin before it returns home.[6]

Engraved on a glass egg by a Russian artist, this souvenir was for sale on the Antarctic tourist ship *Polar Pioneer*.

In some large cities, such as Sydney, Australia, and Boulders near Cape Town, South Africa, colonies of penguins survive, or in the case of Boulders have grown, looked after by concerned citizens, who consider these animals an endearing part of the urban landscape and one to be protected from people, domestic pets and the normal infrastructure of urban living. These penguins are wild pets, cared for by the local community, controlled by our perceptions and stories, but living outside the domestic strictures of traditional pets, such as cats and caged birds. In Manly, Sydney, the penguins are feted as well as protected; their stories are published in sentimental terms in the local media. Individuals, particularly the young, are given names and in some cases wardens – local citizens concerned about the welfare of the colony – are appointed to assist with the care of the colony. Ironically, the exact location of the Little penguin colony is kept secret, a social token of knowledge given only to the privileged and initiated.

Twenty-five years ago penguins were common along Sydney's northern beaches, and residents of beachside suburbs would place chicken wire underneath their houses to keep out the penguins. Locals recall camping on the beach at Manly in the

The Yellow-eyed penguin, a rare species found only in New Zealand and celebrated as a national symbol on the country's $5 note.

1950s and watching the penguins as they walked through the campsite, apparently unconcerned at the intrusion on their beach. The inevitable damage caused by people, their pets and buildings left a much-reduced population at Manly. Five hundred of these penguins were shot in the 1950s and others were killed by dogs. In 1990 one resident became alarmed that the foreshore would be sold to private builders and thus block even further the penguins' access to their nests. He contacted Taronga Zoo, National Parks and Wildlife Service, Maritime Services Board and Manly Council to save the remaining colony. When he did so he was shocked to find out that many residents and the local council had no idea of the penguins' existence.

A management committee was convened and protection began. When in 1995 dogs killed eight birds, further protection work found that a sea wall, built in 1986, had cut off access to part of the colony and that the birds had been using flights of stairs to get to and from the beach to their nests. Now, despite some local opposition, the penguins are protected by local laws and public watchfulness. The Foundation for National Parks and Wildlife has a 'backyard buddies' programme that encourages watchful and careful behaviour near the urban colony. A more protective attitude is perhaps best demonstrated by the headline of the populist *Daily Telegraph*, responding to the smashing of two penguin eggs by vandals: 'Brainless Idiots'.[7]

The 'penguin parade', the daily return journey of penguins from their nests to the sea and back, is now an established tourist venture in Australia. The Little penguin parade has been commercialized at Phillip Island in the state of Victoria. The parade features in travel writing, where the penguins are given the full treatment as little humans – 'the celebrities of the island', one writer declared, adding 'the throngs of visitors coming down to the shoreline penguin parade, to watch these stars come

out, is proof of the deep fascination they hold'.[8] It began as a small operation of a few people watching the return with a torch. Following concern about the decline in penguin numbers in the early 1980s, an Australian Bicentennial Project grant equivalent to US$2.5 million enabled construction of infrastructure to support high-volume tourist traffic. This includes boardwalks across the dunes, an elaborate Visitor Interpretation Centre – incorporating a cafeteria, shop, interactive computer game and a viewing structure, tiered seats accommodating about 3,000 people. In 1995 there were more than 500,000 visitors. An observer described the parade theatrically:

King penguins are the mascot of the Norwegian King's Guard.

> As the final light of the sun left the beach, the crowd hushed to a murmuring, before a North American voice called out. 'Here they come off to the right!' People's

A Penguin Crossing sign, a wildlife warning notice to protect colonies near urban developments.

voices remained low but were coiled with excitement. A ranger announced the first arrivals and repeated the message prohibiting flashlights. Tourists began pointing, as small groups of birds came to shore in various spots. Someone said: 'Here's a bunch, right in front of us.' Another visitor was using night vision video lens, laughing as the penguins waddled up the beach. After about half an hour, penguins emerged in quite large rafts, closer to the lights. . . . As the tourists returned along the boardwalks, domestic scenes were played out around the burrows. It was possible to imagine tiffs, jealous rivalries, rejections and shifting sexual liaisons as penguins huffed and retreated and squatted near their burrows.[9]

A dollar value has been placed on this resource. The 3,000 penguins that make up the show have been valued at US$20,000 each. The penguins (or, more specifically, the people who pay to see the parade) contribute almost US$75 million to the economy of Victoria. The penguin parade advertises itself in two ways. The first offers penguins as 'appealing stars of the theatre of nature', indicated by the name 'Parade'. The second is environment penguin. To participate in the viewing of the parade is also to participate in a natural process – it is a 'way to get back to nature'.[10]

Of the many penguin characters that have emerged in this period, some stand out. In 1986 Otmar Gutman created the animation *Pingu*. *Pingu* began life as a series of five-minute shorts about a mischievous penguin, with a careless disregard for danger. Pingu 'speaks' Pinguinese. It is now a very popular series, which prompted the United States television star David Hasselhoff to release, in Switzerland, a single, *The Pingu Dance*.

The story in literature is more exciting. The Russian novelist Andrey Kurkov wrote two darkly comic novels about the main character, Viktor, and his pet, an emperor penguin called Misha, who has been given the heart of a child. Viktor's world is bleak, not quite loveless, but remote, and, like most pets, Misha provides security in their relationship. In *Penguin Lost* Misha has been kidnapped. The scene of the reunion between Viktor and

Pingu, a popular cartoon character for children.

Misha was described by one reviewer as 'Delicious . . . when Viktor finally finds Misha it is as if Woody Allen had gone to meet Kurtz' – a fittingly apt description and mix of modern characters to describe the reunion of a pet penguin, kept in a compound and with a child's heart beating inside it, with its owner, tired, lonely and dogged, bent on finding his 'pet' and returning it to the wild:

Viktor stood alone in the falling snow, hardly daring to breathe, rooted almost tree-like to the spot, with five Alsatians regarding him from their kennels. If one charged, the others would follow. Had he time to escape? . . . But the dogs had not charged.

Out of the corner of his eye, he saw something move. Without turning his head, he squinted to the uttermost, and saw, waddling to a food bowl by the kennels, a penguin. Bending it picked something from the bowl. It wasn't at all like Misha. It was some other penguin, shorter, thinner.

'Misha!' he called softly, all else forgotten, and the penguin looked at him through the falling snow . . .

The penguin took several steps towards him, stopped, fixed him with his tiny button eyes for a while, then advanced and stared up at him.

Seeing the dogs still sitting or standing, Viktor took a deep breath and slowly eased himself down to the penguin's level.

The penguin came closer.

Heedless now of the dogs, Viktor reached out, stroked its breast, and feeling a long scar, knew at last that it was Misha.[11]

At the end of the novel Misha is released back into the colder seas near an Antarctic island. Kurkov's penguin is no stereotypal clown – if anything, Misha is a source of affection and contact in an often mean and meaningless world. Not comical but an oddity, without commentary but with character and mystery.

In the digital world the Linux penguin trademark appears regularly. Like the Penguin logo, it has its own website and recorded history. It was chosen in early 1996 by Linus Torvalds, the father of Linux, as a suitable logo for the Linux operating system; sharks and eagles were among the other suggestions. The first drawings show a penguin holding up the world. On 9 May 1996 Torvalds sent an email to the designers:

> This one looks like the penguin is not really strong enough to hold up the world, and it's going to get squashed. Not a good, positive logo, in that respect. . . . Now, when you think about penguins, first take a deep calming breath, and think 'cute'. Go back to 'cuddly' for a while (and go on breathing), and then think 'contented' . . .
>
> Then we can do a larger version with some more detail (maybe leaning against a globe of the world, but I don't think we really want to give any 'macho penguin' image here about Atlas or anything).[12]

In 2005 *La Marche de L'Empereur* was released, followed shortly by the English version. *March of the Penguins* was a very successful film, attracting generally ecstatic reviews and winning the Oscar for Best Documentary in 2006. It was the second most viewed documentary in American history, behind *Fahrenheit 9/11*. The film shows the extraordinary breeding cycle of the emperor penguin. In a sometimes cloying and shamelessly

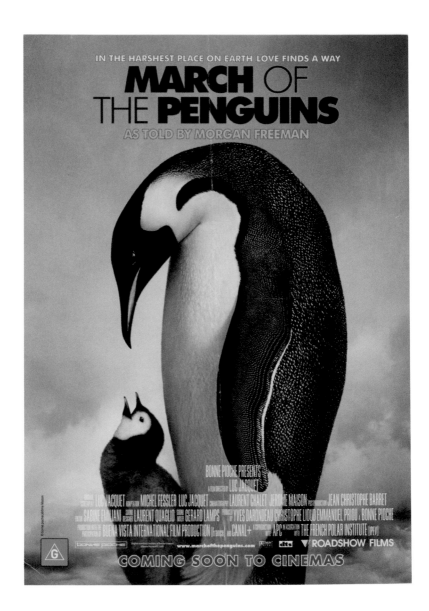

anthropomorphic commentary, the United States actor Morgan Freeman explains the trials of the bird. At the beginning of the movie he explains that it is a film about love: 'This is the incredible true story of a family's journey to bring life into the world . . . In the harshest place on Earth, love finds a way.'[13] He then goes on to relate the mating habits of the Antarctic penguins and their care for the chicks: 'It's an extraordinary pattern of behaviour, worthy of respect and overawe.' Filmed under very difficult conditions by Jérôme Maison and Laurent Chalet at an Emperor penguin colony near the French Antarctic base of Dumont d'Urville, *March of the Penguins* is a beautiful and powerful movie about animal endurance in a very hostile environment.

But it was also subject to manipulation. Perhaps because of the attractiveness of the photography and the appeal of the story and its actors, *March of the Penguins* quickly became a modern fable for groups determined to instil a fundamentalist Christian and anti-evolutionary message into this nature film. Conservative groups in the United States turned the stirring depiction of the Emperor penguin breeding cycle into a 'battle anthem for the culture wars', as Jonathan Miller noted in the *New York Times*.[14] According to the conservative film critic and radio host Michael Medved, *March of the Penguins* was 'the motion picture this summer that most passionately affirms traditional norms like monogamy, sacrifice and child rearing'. He added: 'this is the first movie conservatives have enjoyed since the *Passion of the Christ*. This is *The Passion of the Penguins*.'[15] This was in the context of a wider political struggle between scientists and groups of fundamentalist Christians who were struggling to introduce creationism and the concept of 'intelligent design' into society in general and schools in particular. Churches block-booked sessions. In August 2005 journalist Rich Lowry told a meeting of young conservatives: 'You have to

Emperor penguin as protective father. A striking poster for the very popular Oscar-winning documentary *March of the Penguins*.

check out *March of the Penguins*. It is an amazing movie. And I have to say, penguins are the really ideal example of monogamy. These things – the dedication of these birds is just amazing.'[16] What is equally amazing is that the film simply does not promote monogamy. The narration states that the Emperor penguin is 'monogamous – almost', and that the male and female find new partners every season. So our penguin is misrepresented again. In the interview with Jonathan Miller, Luc Jacquet noted: 'my intention was to tell the story in the most simple and profound way and to leave it open to any reading'. A wise and diplomatic view. The American distributors of the film, Warner Independent Pictures and National Geographic Feature Films, insist that the movie is simply about penguins.[17]

This was not the first time that people had admired the endurance of the Emperor penguin. Films, television shows and magazine articles had explained their story. By the time that David Attenborough retold the story in the BBC series *Life in the Freezer* (1993), it was well known. *March of the Penguins*, the Oscar and the publicity that followed launched the Emperor penguin into international stardom. But penguin became more than a religious political football and world-wide movie star. It moved into a symbol for gender politics: its mating (or perhaps pairing) habits an allegory for justifying human behaviour. News of a zookeeper's plans to introduce female Humboldt penguins (from Sweden) to four non-productive penguins at Zoo am Meer in Bremerhaven in Germany to determine the penguin's sex 'outraged' gay rights activists. 'Gay groups worldwide have been cursing us since the announcement', said the director, Heike Kueck. She continued: 'We don't know whether the three male pairs are really homosexual or whether they have just bonded because of a shortage of females.' The gay rights groups insisted that penguins had a right to form couples without

We're all on thin ice.

human interference; in response, she added: 'Nobody here wants to forcibly separate homosexual couples.'[18]

In New York the debate about homosexual penguins took a similar turn, but with added evidence. A *New York Times* article about same-sex behaviour between animals, 'The Love That Dare Not Squeak Its Name', stimulated the authors, Justin Richardson and Peter Parnell, to write a children's book, *And Tango Makes Three*.[19] This told the story of two male Chinstrap penguins (Roy and Silo) that successfully hatched and raised a chick. The authors were aware that the notion of two gay penguins striving to raise a child would prove controversial and tried to prepare for adverse criticism by making the story as accurate as possible, making several visits to a zoo. They emphasized that 'this actually happened', adding: 'We didn't want to put thoughts and feelings into the heads of the penguins.'[20] Roy and Silo,

A wonderful, evocative use of penguins on this postcard developed for the Australian Conservation Foundation's tour of the film *March of the Penguins*.

157

Gloria, from the
animated film
Happy Feet (2006).

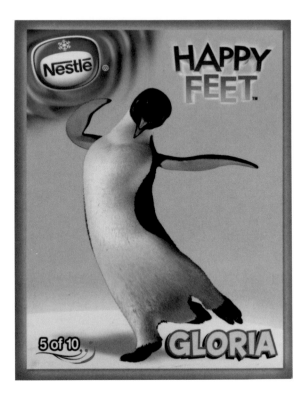

Chinstrap penguins in the real world, became teaching aids in another.[21] As one United States psychiatrist noted: 'One of the areas that parents find very difficult to discuss with their children is homosexuality . . . yet many children have classmates who live in families with two Dads for example.' Parnell's and Richardson's editor at Simon & Schuster in America, David Gale, commented that the book 'never talks about anything more than two penguins that bond and look after a chick'. He reported that sales rose after each challenge to the book and the subsequent publicity.[22]

Penguins were at the peak of international fame when the animated movie *Happy Feet* was released in 2006 by the makers of the popular and financially successful *Babe* movies, George Miller and Associates. Since the 1940s nature films, such as those of Walt Disney's *True Life Adventures*, had made reference to the habitat destruction that often accompanies human activity. *Happy Feet* continued that tradition, using penguins as messengers. This time an animation used endearing penguins that sang and danced – a direct link back to the vaudevillian creatures of Hurley and Ponting. *Happy Feet* tells the story of Mumble, an Emperor penguin, who could not sing as well as the others, but was able to tap dance. Through his journey of excommunication, self-realization and return, Mumble gains knowledge of the environmental destruction of the world by humans – that is, the dangers of overfishing. Mumble and his band of penguin friends are not simply happy-go-lucky singers and dancers, but in their accessible style bring unwelcome news both to the Emperors and to the watching audience. The friends are enacting an age-old, courtly and theatrical role, that of the fool, jesting at the court of international popularity. In his funny, endearing and non-threatening manner, Mumble could safely bring bad news to an authorative figure. The film was very successful, winning an Oscar for best animated feature and achieving world-wide distribution.

Happy Feet had its origins in the BBC series *Life in the Freezer*, which George Miller appreciated for its portrayal of the life cycle of Emperor penguins: 'The way they shared the warmth was a fantastic allegory for how we are as human beings – the better side of us . . . I thought, there's a story here.' Miller, who also made the Mad Max films (known as Road Warrior in the USA), said that there was no difference from a story perspective:

ПОКУПАЙТЕ
МОРОЖЕНОЕ
ГЛАВХЛАДОПРОМА

What I find myself inevitably looking at is the hero myth. I can't help it. I never intended to make Mumble fit any model. But the story emerged as we worked the story and massaged it. I turned around and said not only is it an accidental musical, it pretty much well conforms to the classic hero myth. That's no difference from *Mad Max* or *Babe*.

The process of making the film was complicated and time-consuming. The journey from actor to animated penguin was a long and tortuous one, which began with a process called motion capture. In *Happy Feet* each main character required a dancer, actor and voice. Actors and dancers dressed in black costumes with reflective markers on points of the body: knees, shoulders, wrists and ankles were filmed in action. Cameras tuned to pick up the reflective points, captured the action, and then the film was digitized. The resultant information was used to develop a 'rig', a sort of stylized penguin framework, which animators adapted to suit the purpose of the script. This included features such as expressive movement, facial changes and changes to the beak to match dialogue. The penguin authority, Dr Gary Miller ('Dr Penguin'), advised the actors and dancers on penguin behaviour and movement, and also helped to audition dancers (he had been a dancer himself in his student days). When the characters strayed too far from penguin behaviour – apart from the singing and dancing sequences – he would push for accuracy: 'Basically I was a penguin teacher . . . But my role evolved into being the conscience of real life.'[23]

Penguins, the makers noted in a talk to a packed audience at the State Library of New South Wales, 'all look the same', and since cartooning 'lends itself to characters', an immediate issue was how to develop individual characteristics for them. Anthropomorphism, a time-honoured technique for cartooning and

'Buy ice-cream!', a poster advertising a popular Russian brand.

Magellanic penguin as jailbird: the Presidio de Ushuaia, Tierra del Fuego, was the local gaol from 1902 to 1947. It is now the Museo Maritimo y Museo Del Presidio.

PRESIDIO DE USHUAIA

TIERRA DEL FUEGO

1902 – 1947

animation, was a deliberate choice. At George Miller's suggestion, the 'three amigos' – the three Adélie penguins – were eventually portrayed as Latinos, appealing to the popular notion of Latin Americans as attractive and sensuous dancers. Latino comics did the voices. A cute marketable penguin was also a useful character for the film. The penguin Ramon was given a fluff Mohawk – a reference to the residue of fluff left as the penguin loses its chick covering.[24] Underwater sequences were also created, showing the penguins as fast and graceful swimmers, moving in harmony and precision, thus transforming them suddenly from jester to underwater ballet dancers. This change was not unprecedented in movies: one sequence, not released with the final edition, shows the penguins moving into the routines reminiscent of the Busby Berkley movies of the 1930s.

The penguin transition to cute animated character is almost complete in the animated mockumentary *Surf's Up* of 2007, which features a range of penguins, many of them living on the tropical island of Pen Gu, the 'surf capital of the world' (Hawaii). They surf a lot. Cody Maverick, a young rockhopper penguin that has learnt surfing in Antarctica, wins glory in a competition. The film is more about surfing than penguins, and its central message is of the effort required to reach self-realization; in fact, the characters could be marmosets without any change to the effect of the plot or characterization. In a last link to reality in this sort of use of penguins, Antarctica is a penguin homeland, a place where parents remain while the adventurous youth move into the world. As Cody prepared for his challenge, the

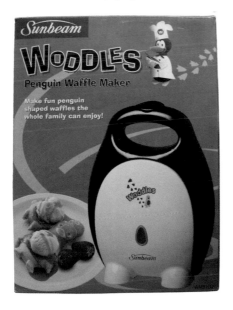

Even the waffles are penguin shaped! The instructions for Sunbeam's waffle maker carry a faintly sinister alert: 'Never leave your penguin waffle maker unattended.'

champ surfer penguin, Tank, told him: 'You should have stayed in Antarctica, son!'[25]

The penguin in all species and forms remains as a significant presence on the Internet, with frequently visited sites devoted to penguin cartoons, penguin natural history, penguin lore and penguin fantasies. Online shops specialize in penguin-related products. Travel sites feature penguins. Club Penguin is an online game for children, in which they can design on-screen penguins. Participants play the role of penguins in particular settings and circumstances; they can also buy a pet. In this world, penguins are cute, harmless and entertaining.

Back in the real world, penguins remain as established symbols of tourism, scientific endeavour and environmental concern, and as a rallying point for environmental groups. In 2007, as the famous All Blacks and Highlanders rugby union hooker Anton Oliver played his final game in the Super 14 competition, a group dressed as Yellow-eyed penguins bade him farewell. 'That was the CEO and board of the Yellow-eyed Penguin Trust', he said. 'I didn't recognise them until they took off their beaks . . . it's only a matter of time before I don the flippers and get my yellow Mohawk on the go.' Oliver is a patron of the Yellow Eyed Penguin Trust, and his retirement was used as an opportunity to gain publicity for the charity.[26]

Meredith Hooper's latest book, *The Ferocious Summer*, is a passionate book about global warming in Antarctica and the effects of climate change on the penguin communities of the Antarctic Peninsula. It concerns real happenings to real birds and uses them as messengers of the human impact on the environment and our attempts to analyse these changes. Ron Naveen's book *Waiting To Fly: My Escapades with the Penguins of Antarctica* (1999) combines the scientific penguin – as much as possible in a general work – with a fond history of its natural history.

Naveen is a scientist, tour guide and writer. His stories are both fables and carefully written accounts of scientific endeavour. But although he loves the many shades of meaning that have been woven around the bird, in the end he would prefer that we allowed penguins to be themselves.[27]

His hopes are unlikely to be realized. The connection between the bizarre fantasy penguin and reality is often blurred and makes great stories for the media. An almost tribal desire for celebrity and the exotic is exemplified in the eating of rare or endangered animals. Celebrity shock chef Kaz Yamamoto includes Emperor penguins in his menu. Journalist Stephen Lemons watched as Yamamoto cooked an Emperor penguin. Although like many today he felt reluctant about eating Emperor penguin: 'As a professionally adventurous eater, I'm ready and willing to try anything new and exotic. And yet penguins are such endearing animals that it's hard not to feel a little sad over seeing one so quickly dissected and fried up like a barnyard hen.' Apparently penguin is an aphrodisiac too. Yamamoto cooked for Ruth Reichl, editor of *Gourmet* magazine and former *New York Times* food critic: 'I fix her penguin liver pâté with peppercorn and Armagnac. She stay with me the night and we make love for 15 hour, she love pâté so much I love her a long time.'[28]

Yamamoto notes provocatively that he and a friend hunted Emperors in the Antarctic in 2004. While this may be great public relations for sensation-hungry fans, both Lemons and Yamamoto would agree that this is inconsequential compared to the other meanings of the Emperor penguin. The strength and hardiness of this species and the simple fact of its survival against enormous odds tacitly challenge our sense of human superiority. In doing so it touches a sense of fragility or vulnerability. Perhaps this is part of the penguin's attraction. Writing in the 1950s, T. R. Henry alluded to this sense of unease when he generalized on the ultimate lesson to be derived from Emperor penguins:

> Penguins are nature's gentle satire on humanity – the odd, bowing, speechmaking birds are a link over a vast chasm of white years between the twentieth century and the time when Antarctica was a green continent and the first precursors of man had not appeared on earth. . . . The way of the emperor penguin may be the way of the struggling last remnants of mankind as the earth grows cold in some faraway future and the human race must adjust to the change or perish.[29]

If there is an image in this period that typifies the penguin, or that provides us with a sense of reality, it is the one that appears in *Life in the Freezer*. In this scene the male emperor penguins stand huddled in the winter dark, heads down to protect themselves from the bitter and freezing winds. The shape of the group, a mass of hunched individuals, is lit by the electric dance of light from the Aurora Australis – the grace of the natural world.

Conclusion

In 2003 Laura Kim, vice-president of Warner Independent Pictures, exasperated at the furore caused by the different interpretations of *March of the Penguins*, exclaimed somewhat unrealistically: 'You know what? They're just birds.'[1] Anthropomorphism is a way of staying in touch with our humanity, of retaining a sense of companionship and equilibrium in our world. Communicating that anthropomorphism is an essential element of storytelling, a reaffirmation of our success as a species to convey emotions and experiences and to use these as binding elements of our social development. Our stories reflect the world around us and make us what we are. The characters and events that we choose to illustrate these tales have a unique and commonly recognized significance. Over the last 500 years the penguin has become a much loved and malleable symbol of this communication. Now penguins interact with people wherever they live. Still mainly on the geographical edges of our lives, these habitats are increasingly threatened with damaging change, and some species are themselves endangered. Penguins continue to provide people with a wealth of information and story.

We have constructed a new set of penguins. They are almost a new species, technologically cloned for our use and entertainment. From the first references of penguins as childlike to the variety on offer today, penguins have moved into our cultural

Crested penguins illustrated by John Gould in *The Birds of Australia* (1840–48).

lives as significant and entertaining symbols. In one sense penguins have come in from the margins, away from the remote geographical spaces into this new cyber world as an even more accessible, and in some cases stranger, creature. In a lineage that stemmed from the aggressive Rockhopper, through the battle stories such as those of Walter Haybittle, penguins now possess an evil connotation in their own right. No longer simple, innocent creatures, the range of penguin representations includes the true incarnation of evil – the antichrist figure of Danny DeVito's character in *Batman Returns*, or the larrikin machine-gun toting birds in *Futurama*, with a battle cry of 'if it ain't black and white, scratch, peck and bite'.[2] The human contact with penguin and its many new forms shows no sign of weakening. Long may this continue.

The final penguin story is that of Billy, the Erect-crested penguin that in 1910 made its appearance on a beach in Lorne, Victoria, Australia. A group of cray fishermen found the penguin and captured it, keeping it in a sea bath for six weeks. During the first two weeks, the penguin was very aggressive, but afterwards it calmed down and became tame. It was called Billy because it rushed eagerly to feed when it heard the sound of a stick being rattled against the billy can that held the small fish on which it fed. One morning Billy followed some bathers to the beach and cautiously followed them into a heavy surf. They called out to the penguin, encouraging it to follow them into deeper water. Billy was knocked over by the waves several times but, gaining confidence, swam swiftly towards the bathers. Dr Nicholls takes up the story:

> Once in the breakers the bird had all the best of it, and we dived and chased him through the waves as one might romp with a dog ashore. Tiring of the sport, Billy commenced to dive and hunt for fish and gradually went out to sea. We called to him by name, and, turning his head, he answered once or twice with a loud squawk, but kept paddling oceanwards all the time. He had suddenly realised that he was once again in the open ocean. The sea had called to him and he had obeyed.[3]

Penguin Species

ADÉLIE penguin (*Pygoscelis adeliae*) is the little black and white penguin of Antarctica that most of us know. It breeds along the Antarctic Peninsula and around most of the perimeter of the continent. Because it breeds further south than any other penguin species (77° s), it spends the least amount of time at its nesting colony, just four to five months each year. For the rest of the time it is at sea, along the northern edge of the pack ice.

AFRICAN penguin (*Spheniscus demersus*), probably the first penguin sighted by Europeans, is the only penguin found in Africa, and it breeds mainly on inshore islands along the southern coast of South Africa as far north as the south-western coast of Namibia. It is a year-round resident.

CHINSTRAP penguin (*Pygoscelis Antarctica*) is the second most abundant penguin on earth. Ninety-five per cent of the birds breed on the islands of the Scotia Arc, especially on the South Sandwich Islands. The Chinstrap is absent from its colony from May to September and presumably disperses to the northern edge of the Antarctic pack ice.

Chinstrap penguin and chicks, Seal Island.

Emperor penguin chick, Cape Washington, Antarctica.

EMPEROR penguin (*Aptenodytes forsteri*) is the only penguin that may never touch land in its lifetime, remaining at sea on pack ice and floes. The most cold-adapted of the seventeen species, it breeds along the Antarctic coast in 42 known colonies, all but five of which are within the Antarctic Circle and none north of 60° s.

ERECT-CRESTED penguin (*Eudyptes sclateri*) lives mainly on two clusters of islands southeast of New Zealand – the Antipodes and the Bounty Islands. They are the main breeding areas of the erect-crested penguin, although some birds also nest on the nearby Auckland Islands. In common with most of the other eudyptid penguins, the Erect-crested vacates its colonies in the winter and is absent from May to September.

FIORDLAND penguin (*Eudyptes pachyrhynchus*) nests only along the south-western coast of New Zealand.

From the top:
Fiordland penguin,
Erect-crested
penguin and
Yellow-eyed
penguin.

Three stages
in the life of a
King penguin,
from a downy
chick to a juvenile
whose moulting
is completed to
an adult rich
in golden
pigment.

GALAPAGOS penguin (*Spheniscus mendiculus*) is the smallest and most tropical of the banded penguins, so called because of the wide stripes around its neck. It is endemic to the Galapagos Islands. The birds remain on the islands throughout the year and breed mainly on Fernandina and the western and northern coasts of Isabella, where the rich up-welling of the cold Cromwell Current supports the population.

GENTOO penguin (*Pygoscelis papua*) is the largest of the brush-tailed group. It breeds on most of the sub-Antarctic islands, from the Falklands east to Macquarie, but it is absent from all the island groups south of New Zealand. This is the northern Gentoo. The other sub-species, the southern Gentoo, nests in the islands of the Scotia Arc and on the Antarctic Peninsula as far south as Petermann Island, at 65°10' s, just short of the Antarctic Circle. At most of the breeding colonies, some birds are present throughout the year.

HUMBOLDT penguin (*Spheniscus humboldti*) is sustained by the riches of the current that flows north along the western coast of South America. It breeds along the coastline and on the offshore islands of Chile and Peru, between 33° and 5° s. Adults remain near their colonies all year.

KING penguin (*Aptenodytes patagonicus*) is a bird of the sub-Antarctic, breeding from Cape Horn east to Macquarie Island. There are no colonies south of 60° s.

LITTLE BLUE penguin (*Eudyptula minor*) breeds around the entire perimeter of New Zealand, along the coast of Tasmania and all the southern coast of the Australian mainland. The Little penguin rarely strays from its breeding colony and can be found nearby throughout the year. Six sub-species are recognized, but these are being evaluated.

MACARONI penguin (*Eudyptes chrysolophus*), the stylish dandy of all penguins, is the most abundant penguin in the world. It nests in the South Atlantic and Indian oceans and breeds further south than any other crested penguin, even reaching the Antarctic Peninsula. The main breeding populations are on South Georgia, Iles Crozet, Iles Kerguelen and Heard and Macquarie Islands, each of which has from one to five million breeding pairs. The bird leaves the colony in April or May and usually does not return until October. These penguins have a beautiful yellow crest that falls along the eyebrow line, droops over the eyes and extends past the back of the head, rather like a brush-back hairstyle. They are named for their resemblance to London dandies, who dressed foppishly and wore hairstyles associated with Italian culture.

previous: King penguins, Fortuna Bay, South Georgia.

MAGELLANIC penguin (*Spheniscus magellanicus*) lives along the South American coasts, usually below 30° s. A small breeding population is also found on the Falkland Islands. In winter the Pacific coast birds migrate as far north as Peru, and those along the Atlantic coast move to the offshore waters of Brazil.

ROCKHOPPER (*Eudyptes chrysocome*) is the smallest of the crested penguins, yet it is tolerant of the greatest range of temperatures and, as a result, has the widest distribution of any of the six crested penguins. It breeds between 37° and 53° s throughout the circumpolar subantarctic. It is absent from its breeding islands from April to September, but its winter range is poorly known.

ROYAL penguin (*Eudyptes schlegeli*) breeds only on Macquarie Island, about 1,450 km (900 miles) south-east of Hobart, Tasmania, and roughly halfway between there and the coast of Antarctica. It is absent from Macquarie Island for four months during the height of the austral winter.

SNARES penguin (*Eudyptes robustus*) breeds only on The Snares, a group of islands roughly 200 km (124 miles) south of New Zealand and barely 250 hectares (620 acres) in extent. Set amid forests of giant tree daises, the nesting colonies are empty from May to August while the birds are at sea.

YELLOW-EYED penguin (*Megadyptes antipodes*) nests on Stewart, Campbell and Auckland islands, the sub-Antarctic islands of New Zealand, off South Island. This large penguin is the most endangered of all the species. It is present at its colony throughout the year.

Timeline of the Penguin

EOCENE 40 MYA	OLIGOCENE 30 TO 40 MYA	PLIOCENE 2–3 MYA	40,000 BCE
Many ancestral penguins evolve in warm seas	Species of large penguins known to exist: fossils found in New Zealand and Peru	Penguins first encounter icy seas	In Australasia, South America and South Africa, penguins are used as food, clothing and possibly as pets

1758	1766	1768	1772	*after* 1800
Scientific classification of a penguin (*Spheniscus demersus*, South African penguin) published in Linnaeus's *Systema natura*	Louis Antoine de Bougainville provides a more detailed and affectionate description of the penguins of Falkland Islands than earlier writers	Thomas Pennant describes several species of penguins to the Royal Society in London	James Cook finds penguins on ice and far from known land, changing the prevailing notion that penguins are usually a sign of nearby land	Sealers in the sub-Antarctic islands and near the Peninsula, use penguins for food

1901	1913–14	1919	1935	1938
First international campaigns to stop the use of penguins for oil	Penguins appear in film as 'comedians' and 'possessors' of new lands	The practice of killing penguins for oil is stopped on Macquarie Island	Penguin Books commences trading using a penguin as its logo	*Mr Popper's Penguins*, a children's literature 'classic', first published

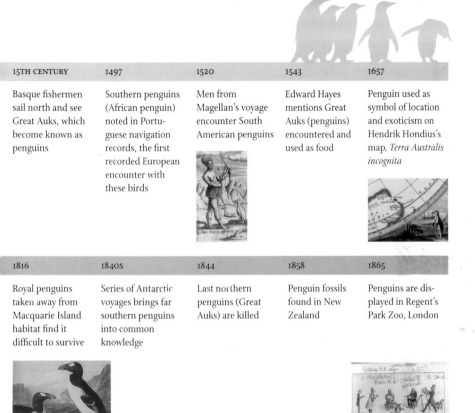

15TH CENTURY	1497	1520	1543	1657
Basque fishermen sail north and see Great Auks, which become known as penguins	Southern penguins (African penguin) noted in Portuguese navigation records, the first recorded European encounter with these birds	Men from Magellan's voyage encounter South American penguins	Edward Hayes mentions Great Auks (penguins) encountered and used as food	Penguin used as symbol of location and exoticism on Hendrik Hondius's map, *Terra Australis incognita*

1816	1840S	1844	1858	1865
Royal penguins taken away from Macquarie Island habitat find it difficult to survive	Series of Antarctic voyages brings far southern penguins into common knowledge	Last northern penguins (Great Auks) are killed	Penguin fossils found in New Zealand	Penguins are displayed in Regent's Park Zoo, London

1941	1986	2000	2003	2006
Oswald Chesterfield Cobblepot first appears in *Detective Comics* as 'The Penguin'; he becomes a regular feature of Batman adventures	Pingu created by Oscar Gutman achieves 'celebrity status' as children's cartoon	Massive operation to clean and evacuate penguins affected by oil spill off South Africa	Penguins taken from Tristan da Cunha to zoos, provoking an international campaign to focus awareness on depleting stocks	*Happy Feet* wins Academy Award for Best Animated Feature; main character, Mumble confirms penguin role for humour and affection

References

INTRODUCTION

1 W. H. Bickerton, 'The Home of the Penguins of the World', *Pall Mall Magazine* (November 1897), pp. 363–9.

2 William L. Fox, *Terra Antarctica: Looking into the Emptiest Continent* (San Antonio, TX, 2005), p. 257; George Gaylord Simpson, *Penguins: Past and Present, Here and There* (New Haven, CT, 1976), p. ix; Diane Ackerman, 'White Lanterns', in *The Moon by Whale Light* (New York, 1991), p. 239.

3 John Winter, quoted in Richard Hakluyt, *Divers Voyages Touching the Discoverie of America and the Islands Adjacent* [1582] (facsimile, Amsterdam, 1967), vol. VIII, p. 96.

4 Peter Cosier, *One Summer Dream* (2007); Katherine West to author, 23 November 2007.

5 Edward A. Wilson, *Report on Mammals and Birds*, National Antarctic Expedition, 1901–4 (London, 1907), vol. II: *Aves*, p. 23.

6 Flip Byrnes, 'In the Footsteps of Frank', *Sydney Morning Herald* (26 August 2007), p. 22.

7 Emile Racovitza, quoted in Ron Naveen, *Waiting to Fly: My Escapades with the Penguins of Antarctica* (New York, 1999), pp. 138–9.

8 Ackerman, 'White Lanterns', p. 192.

9 Quoted in Daphne Guiness, 'A Guy's Guide to Modern Style', *Sydney Morning Herald* [Essential section] (15 November 2007), p. 14.

10 Ackerman, 'White Lanterns', p. 240.

11 Bernard Stonehouse, quoted in Wayne Lynch, *Penguins of the World* (London, 1997), p. 121.

12 Graham Billing, *Forbush and the Penguins* (Wellington, NZ, 1965).
13 Andrey Kurkov, *Death and the Penguin* (London, 2001).
14 Edward Hayes, quoted in Jeremy Gaskell, *Who Killed the Great Auk?* (Oxford, 2000), p. 44.
15 William Jones Rhees, *An Account of the Smithsonian Institute* (Washington, DC, 1857), p. 67.
16 Sir George Peckham, quoted in Hakluyt, *Divers Voyages*, vol. VI, p. 58.

1 PENGUIN FACTS ON FILE

1 T. H. Huxley in Ron Naveen, *Waiting to Fly: My Escapades with the Penguins of Antarctica* (New York, 1999).
2 Julia Clarke, quoted in James Randerson, 'Penguin Ancestor Revealed', *Sydney Morning Herald* (27 June 2007), p. 12; 'Peruvian Prehistoric Penguins were Taller than Danny DeVito', *Scientific American* (25 June 2007): http://blog.sciam.com/index.php?title=peruvian_prehistoric_penguins_were_tall&more [accessed June 2006].

2 VOYAGES OF DISCOVERY

1 Walter Lawry Buller, *A History of the Birds of New Zealand* (London, 1873), p. 276.
2 Anonymous, quoted in George Gaylord Simpson, *Penguins: Past and Present, Here and There* (New Haven, CT, 1976), p. 3.
3 Antonio Pigafetta, *The First Voyage Round the World by Magellan . . .* (London, 1874).
4 Thomas Cavendish, quoted in Richard Hakluyt, *Divers Voyages Touching the Discoverie of America and the Islands Adjacent* [1582] (facsimile, Amsterdam, 1967), vol. VIII, p. 211; p. 305.
5 Sir Richard Hawkins, quoted in John Sparks and Tony Soper, *Penguins* (Sydney, 1967), p. 161.
6 Oliver van Noort, quoted in ibid., p. 163.
7 William Lodewijckszoon, quoted in ibid., p. 164.

8   Sir Thomas Roe, quoted in ibid.

9   Sir John Narborough, *An Account of Several Voyages to the South and North* . . . [1694] (facsimile, Amsterdam, 1969), pp. 24, 58.

10 George Edward, *A Natural History of Birds* . . . , 4 vols (1743–4), p. 49.

11 'Continuation of a Voyage to the South Seas, under the Command of Commodore Anson', *Penny London Post* (26 October 1744).

12 Louis Antoine de Bougainville, quoted in Sparks and Soper, *Penguins*, p. 168.

13 Thomas Pennant, 'An Account of the Different Species of the Birds, called Pinguins', *Philosophical Transactions of the Royal Society*, LVIII (1768), pp. 91–9.

14 Joseph Banks, 'Account of New Zealand', *Endeavour Journal* (August 1768–July 1771), Safe 1/12–13 SLNSW.

15 William Wales, *Journal on the* Resolution, *1 June 1772–17 October 1774* (26 December 1772), Safe 1/84, State Library of New South Wales.

16 Charles Clerke, '30 December 1772', in J. C. Beaglehole, *The Journals of Captain James Cook: The Voyage of the* Resolution *and* Discovery, *1776–1780* (Cambridge, 1967), p. 69.

17 William Wales, '29 December 1772', in ibid.

18 Robert Cooper, '2 January 1775', in ibid., p. 606 ; Joseph Gilbert, '2 January 1775', in ibid., p. 69; Charles Clerke, '3 January 1775', in ibid., p. 615.

19 In Johan R. Forster, *A Voyage Around the World, in His Britannic Majesty's Sloop,* Resolution, *Commanded by Capt. James Cook, during the Years 1772, 3, 4 and 5* (London, 1777).

20 James Cook, quoted in Sparks and Soper, *Penguins*, p. 177.

21 William Frederick Martyn, *Elements of Natural History* (London, 1775).

22 William Clayton, 'An Account of the Falkland Islands', *The Times* (9 November 1775).

23 Charles Taylor, ed., *George Cartwright and his Labrador Journal* (London, 1911), p. 55.

3 SEALERS AND ZOO COLLECTORS

1 *Sydney Gazette* (13 January 1816), p. 2.

2 Augustus Earle, *A Narrative of Nine Months Residence in New Zealand, in 1827, Together with a Journal of Residence in Tristan d'Acunha* (Oxford, 1966), 'Macaroni', p. 228; 'rookery visit', pp. 238–9.

3 Edmund Fanning, quoted in John Sparks and Tony Soper, *Penguins* (Sydney, 1967), pp. 180–81.

4 Thomas Bone (attrib.), *Literary Gazette and Journal of Belle Lettres* (2 November 1821), p. 692.

5 Captain Robert Fildes, *Log of the* Cora, Adm 55/143 supp. Series 11, The National Archives, London, 1599, piece 143, p. 65.

6 Charles Darwin, *Journal of Researches into the Natural History & Geology of the Countries Visited during the Voyage of HMS Beagle* (London, 2005), p. 198.

7 Joseph-Fidèle-Eugène Dubouzet, in Dumont d'Urville, 'The Journal of Dumont d'Urville', in *Antarctic Manual*, ed. George Murray (London, 1901), p. 447.

8 James Clark Ross, *A Voyage of Discovery and Research in the Southern and Antarctic Regions* (London, 1847), p. 234.

9 William Reynolds, *Voyage to the Southern Ocean: Letters of Lieutenant William Reynolds from the US Exploring Expedition, 1838–1842* (Annapolis, MD, 1988), Letter no. 14, March 1840, p. 131.

10 'The Zoological Gardens Regent's Park', *The Times* (18 April 1865), p. 10.

11 'Dye and Diet', *West Coast Times* (12 March 1877).

12 W. L. Buller, *Birds of New Zealand*, 2nd edn (London, 1888), p. 303.

13 Ibid.

14 W. L. Buller, 'Notes and Observations on New Zealand Birds', *Transactions and Proceedings of the New Zealand Institute*, XXIV (1891), pp. 71–2.

15 'A Nice Bird for Baby', *West Coast Times* (24 February 1880), p. 2.

16 Alfred Newton, ed., *A Dictionary of Birds*, 1 vol. in 2 (London, 1893–6), p. 215.

17 Ibid., p. 706.

18 Ibid., p. 471.
19 'Belle Vue Gardens', *Manchester Times* (8 June 1889).
20 Uncle Old Man, 'Crozet Joe: The Story of Adventure', *Manchester Times* (9 November 1894).
21 W. G. Burn Murdoch, *From Edinburgh to the Antarctic: An Artist's Notes and Sketches during the Dundee Antarctic Expedition of 1892–93* [1894] (Bungay, Suffolk, 1984), p. 230.

4 ANTARCTICA TO ANIMATION

1 Louis Gain, quoted in Ron Naveen, *Waiting to Fly: My Escapades with the Penguins of Antarctica* (New York, 1999), p. 139.
2 Edward A. Wilson, *Report on Mammals and Birds,* National Antarctic Expedition, 1901–04 (London, 1907), vol. II: *Aves,* p. 38.
3 Ibid., p. 3.
4 Ibid., p. 16.
5 Ibid., p. 11.
6 Ibid., p. 31.
7 'The Destruction of Penguins', *Otago Daily Times* (1 June 1905).
8 Anatole France, *Penguin Island*, trans. A. Evans (London, 1926), pp. 20, 22.
9 Apsley Cherry-Garrard, *The Worst Journey in the World* (Harmondsworth, 1970), p. 282.
10 Ibid., p. 275.
11 Ibid., p. 643.
12 Ibid., p. 625.
13 Ibid., p. 626.
14 Ibid., p. 629.
15 Herbert George Ponting, *The Great White South* (London, 1932), p. 166.
16 Frank Hurley, 'Scope of Polar Photographs', *Australian Photo-Review* (23 March 1914), pp. 129–30.
17 Reviews and notices reprinted on Lee Keedick, 'Movie Poster', *Sir Douglas Mawson's Marvelous Bird, Animal and Travel Motion Pictures* (New York, 1915).

18 Miriam Teichner, 'Charlie Chaplin: A Tragedian Would Be', *New York Globe* (19 February 1916).

19 *Toronto World* (17 August 1915).

20 Ponting, *The Great White South*, p. 247.

21 Frank Hurley, *Sydney Morning Herald* (14 August 1919).

22 Apsley Cherry-Garrard, *The Times* (4 April 1919).

23 Apsley Cherry-Garrard, 'Shall the Penguins Call Us Huns?', *The Spectator* (26 April 1919), p. 521.

24 Apsley Cherry-Garrard, *The Times* (29 December 1919).

25 H. G. Wells, *The Undying Fire: A Contemporary Novel* (New York, 1919), pp. 90–92.

26 Norman Lindsay, *The Magic Pudding: Being the Adventures of Bunyip Bluegum and his Friends Bill Barnacle and Sam Sawnoff* (Sydney, 1918).

27 Paul Carter, *Little America: Town at the End of the World* (New York, 1979), p. 63.

28 Ibid., p. 205.

29 Cherry Kearton, *The Island of Penguins* (London, 1937), p. ix.

30 Ibid., p. 20.

31 Ibid., p. 62.

32 Ibid., p. 86.

33 Ibid., p. 109.

34 Erling Christophersen, *Tristan da Cunha: The Lonely Isle* (London, 1940), p. 89.

35 Ibid., p. 90.

36 Ibid., p. 140.

37 Ibid., p. 142.

38 *The Times* (29 December 1961), p. 4.

39 See, for example, 'Winter Work at the Zoo', *The Times* (29 January 1936).

40 Hitchcock, quoted in *The Times* (5 October 1937), p. 15. For an interesting account, see William Fisher, *The Empty Stage: Berthold Lubetkin's Penguin Pool at London Zoo*, www.rhwl.com/news/RHWL_EssaybyWilliamFisher.pdf [accessed June 2009].

41 T. R. Henry, *The White Continent: The Story of Antarctica* (London, 1950), p. 154.

42 H. K. Lillie, *The Path through Penguin City* (London, 1955), p. 70.

43 Len Hill, *Penguin Millionaire: The Story of Birdland* (London, 1976), p. 93.

44 Willie the KOOL: www.geocities.com/~jimlowe/kool/history.html [accessed February 2006].

45 Penguin books logo at http://www.YouTube.com/watch?v=6h1I_smr38A

46 Quoted in Morine Krissdóttir, *Descents of Memory: The Life of John Cowper Powys* (New York, 2007), p. 242.

47 Henry Miller, *Sexus* (London, 1970), p. 143.

48 Richard Atwater and Florence Atwater, *Mr Popper's Penguins* (Boston, MA, 1938).

49 Max Harris, *Mithridatum of Despair*, Ern Malley: The Official Website, www.ernmalley.com/angry_penguins.html [accessed June 2009].

50 *History of the Munsingwear Penguin*: www.originalpenguin.com/history.html [accessed April 2006].

51 'Mary Poppins, Production 1872, Walt Disney Studios', *A Film Treatment Based on the Stories by P. L. Travers* (28 March 1961), p. 25.

52 Dick Van Dyke, 'Penguin Dance Sing Along': www.youtube.com/watch?v=-nQtRSHKDpg [accessed October 2008].

5 TOURISM, FILMS, FOOD

1 Stephen Murray Smith, *Sitting on Penguins: People and Politics in Australian Antarctica* (Surry Hills, NSW, 1988), p. 34.

2 'Plans to Pick Up Penguins Attacked', *BirdLife International* (28 September 2003): www.birdlife.org/news/news/2003/10/rockhopper.html [accessed June 2007].

3 John Visser, quoted in 'Fury as Dealer Picks Up 240 Wild Penguins', *Guardian Unlimited* (1 March 2004): www.buzzle.com/editorials/1-3-2004-49084.asp [accessed October 2008].

4 Malay environmental spokesman quoted in *Guardian Unlimited* (1 March 2004): www.buzzle.com/editorials/1-3-2004-49084.asp [accessed June 2009].

5 Alan Teh Leam Seng, 'Walking with Penguins', *New Straits Times* (21 December 2004).

6 King penguin pet on YouTube, a site for modern film and entertainment: www.youtube.com/watch?v=1vk9Ka7e4Y8 [accessed June 2009].

7 'Penguin Nest Vandalised', *Daily Telegraph* (7 December 2006).

8 Judith Ellen, 'Little Wonders', *Sydney Morning Herald* (14 April 2007), p. 6.

9 Quoted in Chilla Bulbeck, *Facing the Wild: Ecotourism, Conservation and Animal Encounters* (Sterling, VA, 2005), p. 76.

10 Philip Island advertisements, Travel section, *Weekend Australian* (14–15 April 2007), p. 6.

11 Andrey Kurkov, *Penguin Lost* (London, 2005), p. 161.

12 Linus Torvalds, quoted on www.sjbaker.org/wiki/index.php/ title=The_History_of_Tux_the_Linux_Penguin#Beginnings [accessed October 2008].

13 Morgan Freeman from Luc Jacquet, *March of the Penguins* (Washington, DC, c2006).

14 Jonathan Miller, 'March of the Conservatives: Penguin Film as Political Fodder', *New York Times* (13 September 2005). For a selection of reviews of the film, see www.rottentomatoes.com/ m/march_of_the_penguins [accessed October 2008].

15 Michael Medved, in ibid.

16 Rich Lowry, in ibid.

17 Luc Jacquet, in ibid.

18 Heike Kueck, quoted in 'Gay Outrage over Penguin Sex Test', *BBC News* (14 February 2005): http://news.bbc.co.uk/2/his/europe/ 4264913.stm [accessed June 2007].

19 Dinitia Smith, 'The Love That Dare Not Squeak Its Name', *New York Times* (7 February 2004); Justin Richardson and Peter Parnell, *And Tango Makes Three* (New York, 2005).

20 Quoted in Richard Lea, 'March of the Penguin Protesters',

Guardian Unlimited (23 May 2007): www.guardian.co.uk/books/
2007/may/23/booksforchildrenandteenagers.richardlea
[accessed October 2008].

21 Quoted in ibid.

22 David Gale, quoted in ibid.

23 Gary Miller, quoted in Rosalie Higson, 'In Fantasia's Footsteps',
Weekend Australian (23–4 December 2006), pp. 4–5.

24 *Happy Feet*, seminar at State Library, New South Wales, Sydney,
1 March 2007.

25 Ash Bannon and Chris Buck, dir., *Surf's Up*, Columbia Pictures,
2007.

26 Anton Oliver, quoted in Rupert Guiness, 'You're Better Losers
Than We Are, Says Oliver', *Sydney Morning Herald* [Sport]
(30 June–1 July 2007, p. 67.

27 Meredith Hooper, *The Ferocious Summer* (London, 2007);
Ron Naveen, *Waiting To Fly: My Escapades with the Penguins of
Antarctica* (New York, 1999).

28 Stephen Lemons, 'Xtreme Cuisine', *Phoenix New Times* (11 May
2006).

29 T. R. Henry, *The White Continent: The Story of Antarctica* (London,
1950), p. 144.

CONCLUSION

1 Laura Kim, quoted in Jonathan Miller, 'March of the Conservatives:
Penguin Film as Political Fodder', *New York Times* (13 September
2005).

2 Quoted in 'Bird Bot of Ice-catraz', *Futurama* episode 5, series 3,
Fox Network, 2001.

3 Quoted in A. F. Bassett Hull, 'On the Occurrence of the Crested
Penguin (*Eudyptes chrysocome*) in Australia', *Records of the
Australian Museum* (September 1918), p. 73.

Select Bibliography

Davis, Lloyd Spencer, *Smithsonian Q & A: Penguins, the Ultimate Question and Answer Book* (New York, 2007)
—, and Martin Renner, *Penguins* (New Haven, CT, 2004)
—, and John T. Darby, eds, *Penguin Biology* (San Diego, CA, 1990)
Love, John A., *Penguins* (London, 1994)
Lynch, Wayne, *Penguins of the World* (Kingston, Ontario, Firefly Books, 1997)
Naveen, Ron, *Waiting to Fly: My Escapades with the Penguins of Antarctica* (New York, 1999)
Simpson, George Gaylord, *Penguins: Past and Present, Here and There* (New Haven, CT, 1976)
Sparks, John, and Tony Soper, *Penguins* (Sydney, 1967)

Websites

CLUB PENGUIN
www.clubpenguin.com
A site for children's games.

PENGUIN PLACE
www.penguin-place.com
A site for penguin lovers and shoppers. The site contains an amazing range of penguin tat and information. It includes links to the *Penguin Post*, a newsletter devoted to penguins.

PENGUIN SCIENCE
www.penguinscience.com/
Understanding penguin response to climate and ecosystem change.

SEAWORLD
www.seaworld.org/infobooks/Penguins/home.html
Scientific information about penguins.

See also blog posts about penguins for personal comments and descriptions of people and penguins.

Acknowledgements

Researching and writing a book like *Penguin* has been a rewarding and enjoyable experience. The work was not done alone and many people contributed to the book's development and publication. Jonathan Burt provided essential and considered advice, Suzie Grant and Olwen Pryke also assisted with comments and information. Peter Cosier and Caroline McFarlane of the Wentworth Group of Concerned Scientists were supportive and helpful, as were Jane Reid, Kristen van de Meer and many others. Alan Brightman, Brian Brown and Roger Shehani listened patiently to the many penguin stories I told while we patrolled with the South Narrabeen Surf Life Saving Club. Greg and Margaret Mortimer of Aurora Expeditions and their staff and passengers continued to be interested and engaged with the project – Greg and Margaret's generosity afforded trips south to see penguins in their homelands. Aurora's natural history staff – Santiago Imberti, Roger Kirkwood and Peter Gill – helped out with specific information on penguin behaviours and habitats. Ben Wallis generously gave permission for me to use his striking image of a King penguin swimming as the book's frontispiece. My colleagues at the State Library of New South Wales – Mitchell Librarian Richard Neville, Scott Wajon and Bruce York, who made the beautiful copies of images in the Library's collection – assisted openly and generously. Reaktion staff, including Michael Leaman, Robert Williams and Susannah Jayes, provided comments and advice that have improved *Penguin* in many ways. Finally, I acknowledge the support and patience of my two sons, Tom and Max, who consistently showed interest and patience in my work on *Penguin*.

Photo Acknowledgements

The author and publishers wish to express their thanks to the below sources of illustrative material and/or permission to reproduce it. (Some sources uncredited in the captions for reasons of brevity are also given below.)

Boston Public Library: p. 113; The British Museum: p. 43; Matt Brown: p. 126; C. Harmoney: p. 34; Getty Images: p. 28; Istockphoto: pp. 30 (Rich Lindie), 141 (Dan Kite), 150 (Steven Hayes), 174 (Mlenny Photography); Michael Leaman: p. 132; Steve Martin: pp. 18, 19, 25, 29, 32, 146; Mitchell Library, State Library of New South Wales: pp. 39, 42, 56, 58, 59, 83, 92, 93, 97, 100, 116, 128; National Oceanic & Atmospheric Administration Photo Library, Washington DC: pp. 75 (Archival Photography by Steve Nicklas, NOS, NGS), 106 (Dr Levick), 145 (OAR/National Research Program [NURP]), 79, 89, 96, 101, 109, 122, 136, 142, 171 (top) (Michael Van Woert, NOAA NESDIS, ORA), 171 (bottom) (Lieutenant Philip Hall, NOAA Corps); Penguin Books: p. 135; Jack Pickard: p. 127; Rex Features: pp. 14 (Stock Connection), 38 (Neil Stevenson), 108 (Matthew Power), 133 (Everett Collection), 149 (Tom Kidd); © V&A Images/Victoria and Albert Museum, London: p. 78; Ben Wallis: p. 6; Zoological Society of London: pp. 51, 55.

Index